COME ALIVE—[

- 7 steps to finding your purpose in life
- 7 career stages and how to manage them
- 7 laws of luck and how to make them happen
- 21 exercises of self-discovery
- 3 mythic stories to empower your journey through life
- 3 life stages and how to live them
- 5 things to do if you hit bottom
- 1 thing you do best and would love to do

FINDING THE HAT THAT FITS

How to Turn Your Heart's Desire into Your Life's Work

JOHN CAPLE, a Stanford University graduate who also earned an M.B.A from Harvard, currently conducts workshops on strategic planning for corporate executives. He is a former corporate executive and chairman of the business department of Dominican College of San Rafael, California. His other books include *The Ultimate Interview, Careercycles,* and *The Right Work.* He lives in San Rafael, California.

FINDING THE HAT THAT FITS

How to Turn Your Heart's Desire into Your Life's Work

John Caple, Ph.D.

A PLUME BOOK

PLUME
Published by the Penguin Group
Penguin Books USA Inc., 375 Hudson Street,
New York, New York 10014, U.S.A.
Penguin Books Ltd, 27 Wrights Lane,
London W8 5TZ, England
Penguin Books Australia Ltd, Ringwood,
Victoria, Australia
Penguin Books Canada Ltd, 10 Alcorn Avenue,
Toronto, Ontario, Canada M4V 3B2
Penguin Books (N.Z.) Ltd, 182–190 Wairau Road,
Auckland 10, New Zealand

Penguin Books Ltd, Registered Offices:
Harmondsworth, Middlesex, England

First published by Plume, an imprint of New American Library, a division of Penguin
Books USA Inc.

First Printing, June, 1993
10 9 8 7 6 5 4 3 2 1

Two stanzas from "Vacillation" by William Butler Yeats reprinted with permission of
Macmillan Publishing Company from *The Poems of W. B. Yeats: A New Edition,* edited by
Richard J. Finneran. Copyright 1933 by Macmillan Publishing Company, renewed 1961 by
Bertha Georgie Yeats.

Barzotti cartoon reprinted with permission of *The New Yorker,* 20 West 43rd Street, New
York, NY 10036.

 REGISTERED TRADEMARK—MARCA REGISTRADA

LIBRARY OF CONGRESS CATALOGING-IN-PUBLICATION DATA:

Caple, John,
    Finding the hat that fits : how to turn your heart's desire into
your life's work / John Caple.
      p. cm.
    ISBN 0-452-26996-2
    1. Job satisfaction. 2. Vocational guidance. 3. Career changes.
I. Title.
HF5549.5.J63C346   1993
650.14–dc20   92-40143
                                                           CIP

PRINTED IN THE UNITED STATES OF AMERICA
Set in New Baskerville
Designed by Leonard Telesca

BOOKS ARE AVAILABLE AT QUANTITY DISCOUNTS WHEN USED TO PROMOTE PRODUCTS OR SERVICES.
FOR INFORMATION PLEASE WRITE TO PREMIUM MARKETING DIVISION, PENGUIN BOOKS USA INC., 375
HUDSON STREET, NEW YORK, NEW YORK 10014.

for
Frances Swartzbaugh Caple
who first taught me about
hats and purpose and life

"'I yam what I yam an' tha's all I yam!' What
the hell kind of résumé is that?"

Thank You

Finding the hat that fits is not a solo activity. Nor is writing a book. Both require help, and I have had lots of it—wonderful advice, ideas, support, and encouragement.

I am particularly grateful to Malcolm Brodzinsky, Tom Caple, Tom Day, Dan Druckerman, JoAnn Haymaker, Patti Hoffman, Norwin Joffie, Jay Levinson, Pierre Mornall, Terry Pearce, Denize Springer, Manny Talkovsky, and Rene Tihista who read all or part of early drafts. Dick Bolles, George Conlan, Blair Ogden, Ann Schroeder, Max Shapiro, Kathy Walther, and Karin Winner each helped in their own way.

Special thanks to members—past and present—of my CEO group: Mark Agnew, Biff Barnard, Robin Bradford, Jim Finkelstein, Margot Fraser, Jason Gilman, Rick Green, Peter Gumina, Bruce James, Mike Moore, Andy Pansini, Dennis Sholl, Don Sullivan, Bob Warden, and Randy Zucker.

Huge thanks to Alexia Dorszynski and Deb Brody, my editors at NAL/Dutton, for insight, inspiration, clarity, enthusiasm. To Michael Larsen and Elizabeth Pomada, my literary agents, for making this all happen. And to my wife Anne, for patience, good sense, and for blessing so many humble beginnings by writing, "Looks good to me!"

The biggest thank you of all goes to my many teachers, including—besides those above—coaching and counseling clients, participants in workshops and lectures, and all of you who care enough about living on purpose to pick up this book.

Contents

Introduction

On a steamy July morning John Bednarak and I are sipping coffee in the sales shack of the used car lot at Lownsbury Chevrolet. It's too early for customers and I'm still relishing yesterday's achievement: after three test drives, a local garbage man bought our last Nash Rambler, barely able to ramble, for $50. John has been having a good week, too.

"I can't wait to get down to Florida this winter," he tells me. "I make it in two days, hitchhiking." With his withered left leg, John can barely get across the lot, so I'm wondering how he makes it across five states. Then he tells me, "The secret is my red gas can.

"It came from the hardware store, brand new, and I cut a square piece out of the bottom, put on hinges and a latch to make a little door. I put my shirts and razor in there and stick out my thumb." The picture of little John, standing by the Dixie Highway, excites my travel lust. At 19, with so much of the world yet to see, I can imagine nothing more adventurous. "I never wait more than five minutes," he tells me. "I always get a ride."

That's how I'll get up to Crystal Lake to visit my cousin, I'm thinking; it's just across the line up in Michigan, less than 200 miles. With my red gas can the trip will be a cinch.

That night I buy a five-gallon gas can, hinges, and a latch. By the weekend, I have fashioned a working door in the bottom. In black enamel I paint three large letters on the side, GAS. I feel the joy of a perfect plan.

Since that 1950s summer I have created hundreds of plans and traveled to many parts of the world by car and plane and train and, on occasion, by sticking out my thumb. I have visualized many destinations—some nearby like the cabin at Crystal Lake, some far in the future—and I have undertaken many missions. Along the way I have come to understand my purpose—as I hope you will come to understand yours in the pages ahead. My purpose here is to help you clarify your vision, to see more clearly where you are going. I hope you will better understand your mission—how you aim to get to where you are going—and your purpose, the source of meaning and fulfillment in the journey.

Vision, mission, and purpose are essentials for success in life. Stanford psychologist Jeffery Wildfogel, a student of peak performance, adds another essential: the ability to alter our perception of reality, to adapt new paradigms. "Almost always," says Wildfogel, "breakthroughs in performance require identification of inappropriate paradigms and adoption of new ones."

This book is about vision, mission, and purpose—and invites you to see your world differently, to adapt new mental models in making it all work for you. This book is for those of you who want your work and your life to be more meaningful, valuable, rewarding. That summer at Lownsbury Chevrolet I learned that I never again wanted to promote used cars—or *anything* I don't believe in. This trip we are on is for learning, for discovering what we want and what we don't and how to bring the best of our talent and knowledge and passion to bear in the world—and have fun doing it. This book is for all of us who want our lives to have significance.

The pages before you are built on five basic ideas:

- **Purpose empowers.** To live on purpose is to discover our power, our capacity to add value to our every experience, to the lives of those around us, and to the world.

- **Purpose enables.** Finding and living our life mission adds meaning and dignity to life. Living on purpose is a noble adventure.
- **Purpose liberates.** When we have a sense of purpose, we stop worrying about life direction. We find joy and freedom in each moment. We laugh more and lighten up. We live with love.
- **Purpose changes,** but not often and usually not much. While our insights deepen—as yours will in the chapters ahead—and our expression of these insights becomes more articulate, our core life mission changes little over the years.
- **Purpose emerges in living life.** The first half of this book describes the cycles and rhythms of life—the successes and failures, the joys and heartaches and lessons that illuminate purpose. The second half tells how to make the journey successful. Each experience tells us something about why we are here. Each experience is a chance to live on purpose.

I never took the trip to Michigan with a red gas can in my hand, but I am on a larger trip through the world of love and work. There have been detours for me—side trips, unexpected vistas, and new friends. Along the way I've heard lots of wisdom and many stories, some of which are retold in the pages that follow.

One of these stories—a bit of oriental wisdom for you, for me, for all who search for the right path—is about the Chinese lawgiver Confucius.

At the end of a long and productive career, the story goes, Confucius returned to the village where he was born to spend his remaining days. Late each morning, he would stroll into the town square and sit in the sun with a broad straw hat shading his eyes. The boys of the village would see the slumbering old man and wonder how he had earned his great reputation.

"He's nothing but a doddering old fool," said the leader of the gang. When he saw the other boys smile, he added, "and I can prove it.

"You see this little bird? I'll cover it with my hands and then we'll ask the old fogey if the bird is dead or alive. If he says dead I'll open my hands and the bird will fly away. If he says alive I'll crush it to death with my hands and he'll be wrong again. We can't miss!"

"Rad, man!" the boys chortled. "Awesome!" And off they ran with their leader to the square.

Bowing deeply, the lead boy spoke to Confucius, "Oh honorable master, may I ask you, please, a question?"

Confucius looked up.

"I have here in my hands a bird. Is it alive or is it dead?"

Confucius smiled with great affection and a few missing teeth. Then he said to those boys, as I say to you now, "The answer is in *your* hands."

The only one who can make your work better, or your play, or your life, is you. The only one who can make this book a force for change in your life is you. You hold the key. The power comes from you. The answer is in *your* hands.

PART

I

Seven Steps
to Purpose

1

Starting Out

Your old men shall dream dreams, your
young men shall see visions.

Joel 2:28

Look with favor upon a bold beginning.

—Virgil, *Eclogues*

"Begin at the beginning," the king said,
very gravely, "and go on till you come to
the end: then stop."

—Lewis Carroll, *Alice in Wonderland*

"Dear Bob," the letter begins, "I thought it would never happen,
but I finally got the job I've been dreaming about. It was worth
the endless interviews and rejections. It was worth all the time I
spent analyzing my strengths and researching companies and
calling friends who weren't always so friendly. Even if it had been
twice as hard, this job is absolutely worth it."

Susan's letter goes on to describe a boss "who appreciates my
intellect and loves to delegate" and a workspace that is "aesthet-
ically pleasing, creatively designed, and most important, filled
with sunlight."

How did this all work out? We don't know. It could be that Susan never even got this job, because the words you just read are
from a letter describing a two-years-in-the-future fantasy. It could
also be that she is now doing something that exceeds her
dreams. It could be that her reality today is richer and more fulfilling than her best fantasy ever was.

Fantasy is just one of the ways we start our quest. It can be in a letter like the one here written by a client of mine. It can be a childhood dream or a half-formed image as you worked out this morning. There is more than fantasy to starting out, however, whether you are 16 or 36, whether you are a high school dropout or a Ph.D. in nuclear physics.

Wherever you are in life, whatever your fantasies, there are four essential behaviors for starting successfully on whatever comes next:

- *Explore.* Search out new possibilities for your life. Examine your options for action, even the outrageous ones beyond your current comfort zone. Use the EXPLORATIONS in this book to discover your inner wisdom and uncover the wisdom around you. If you are in school, use class assignments to learn about your motivation and about careers best suited to your passions. You have to do the work anyway, so make it pay off—as I did in eighth grade when I interviewed an architect neighbor to see if I would enjoy that career as much as I imagined (the answer was no). Explore as you continue through this book and keep on exploring in every part of your life. Feel your longings, dream your dreams, refine your fantasies—then explore ways to bring them into reality.

- *Inquire.* Cultivate curiosity in work, in love, and in life. Maintain an inquiring mind. Listen carefully. Be attentive to people and ideas. Learn from audio tapes, videos, books, newspapers—wherever information can be found. Use life experiences to create your future. When I visited my father's cluttered, dusty office as a boy, I learned volumes by listening to him on the phone, observing the farmers who came to see him, and being in that world of small business—a world I still love and learn from.

- *Experiment.* View life as a laboratory and experience (good or bad) as an opportunity to test your hypotheses about the nature of existence—especially *your* existence. As you read this book, try out the ideas that excite you. Be practical, but innovative. Be willing to be surprised and willing to change. It all has value. When I was in college I worked as a gate captain collecting tickets at football games and as a hasher serving food in fraternity houses. While I do neither of those things now, I continue to experiment and I still like to help people get in and get fed.

Success comes to those who integrate exploration, inquiry, and experimentation into their lives. Success comes to those who understand that they work together like intersecting circles:

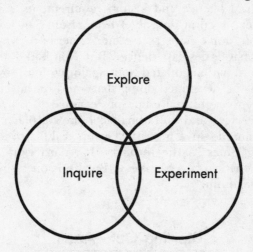

There is a final behavior that all three of the first require and upon which all life depends:

- *Begin.* "Great is the art of beginning," wrote Longfellow, "but greater is the art of ending." Start with the art of beginning. Take small first steps with the sure knowledge that they will lead eventually to the land of your dreams. Take the small first steps to explore, to inquire, to experiment—and you will then know when to take the big steps of accepting your next job or changing careers. As General H. Norman Schwartzkopf says, "Make a decision. Act. Action will bring new information to let you know if you are on course." A business executive I know says it another way: "Do all you can to discover what work is best for you. If you can't figure it out, do something, anything, and it will lead you to what is right."

My son Tom took a year to get started after graduating from the University of Oregon. He explored, he inquired, he experimented, he persevered until he got the commercial real estate job of his dreams. He started while still a student at Eugene, taking courses in real estate finance and real estate law in addition to his political science and history requirements. After graduation he interviewed at dozens of firms, from San Jose to Sacramento. "You don't have real estate experience," he was told. "You don't have sales experience." But Tom had done construction work and had negotiated house-painting jobs, so he focused on the skills he developed doing that—and on his commitment to being a successful real estate professional.

Fifty interviews and hundreds of phone calls later he got the offer he wanted—in a growing Grubb & Ellis office—despite challenging times in the industry. It's hard work, with long hours, and the starting pay is low. But he is on his way. He has made his beginning.

Starting Out—Again

Not long ago Will Haymaker went job hunting. Will graduated from Purdue University many years ago, and at age 62 he has had lots of jobs. He was unsure about starting out again, feeling insecure, and the other participants in the workshop he was taking on "Men, Meaning, and Work" had some advice.

"Be clear about your purpose," they told him. "Be clear about your strengths. Show that at your age you have the experience to know your best skills and the wisdom to use them effectively." Someone said, "Tell them you want to do this job for five years . . . that will show them you are committed." Everyone encouraged him.

"Your coaching got me that job," Will told us later, and perhaps the ideas that helped him will help you. Some other tips for starting out, wherever you are in life:

- *Play "What If?"* On your computer or in your mind play out different scenarios. Look for lots of possibilities before narrowing down your choices. Be creative. Expand your options. Then evaluate and assess before acting.
- *Start at the Top.* Begin with your number-one dream. Don't let a sense of limitations—"I don't have the education," or "I don't have the brains," or "Those jobs are impossible to get"—defeat you at the get-go. Aim to get some part of your dream as you start, even if it is through a series of steps that takes 10 years. You can be happy in low-level jobs if you have high-level dreams. You can be fulfilled doing small tasks if you have big purposes.
- *Make Money.* Add to your bank balance while adding to your store of knowledge. If you are starting out in life, get summer and part-time jobs that pay you to learn. If you are starting out later in life, consider temporary work or consulting during career transitions. (There is also value to working without pay. Internships, Peace Corps assignments, and volunteer projects are great ways to learn.)

This book is about finding your purpose and finding success—what all of us want, no matter what our age. Read on and you will find these things. What is even more important, though, you will find yourself. And in finding yourself you will become the designer of your own future.

As designer of my own future I drove across the United States in a 1950 Chevrolet to spend the summer of my eighteenth year working on a cattle ranch in Wolf Creek, Montana. Romantic images of cowboys and wide open spaces filled my head but what I found was hard living and hard work. The only horses I saw were in the corral I passed driving a tractor out to the hayfields at six o'clock each morning, and the closest I got to cowboys was rooting for bull riders at the Montana State Fair. But I loved the freedom and the learning and the vastness of the Rocky Mountain range country.

That summer in the Big Sky country taught me that I did not want to be a lonely cattle rancher working long hours for low returns. It taught me that I was happier using my brain than my back. That summer helped shape my role in life as a connector, a bridge between worlds, working to link people and ideas in ways that lead to action.

All that follows has been created as part of my role as a connector of people and ideas. That is what this book is about. Every story, every exploration, every success strategy is designed to link you with ideas that make a difference in your life. Every word here is designed to support you in living on purpose.

2

Listen to Your Heart

> Always, from girlhood, I had shaped
> futures with my mind, sculpting them as a
> sculptor shapes clay. Events always altered
> the imaginary shapes I made, but not
> totally. Enough of my construct survived
> that I could at least recognize it.
>
> —Jill Peel, in *Somebody's Darling*
> by Larry McMurtry

> The heart has its reasons that reason can
> not know.
>
> —Pascal, *Pensées*

> If a man does not know his purpose he is
> not alive—he is among the walking dead.
>
> —Michael Meade, storyteller/drummer

Why are we here?

Where are we going?

How do we get there?

What can we do to find the answers to these questions? Shall we consult philosophers? Professors? Theologians? Tibetan wise men in mountain caves?

The truth is that we never find a final answer. We never know if we have it just right. I know that I will have raisin bran and a sliced banana for breakfast tomorrow, and you may know exactly what will be in your bowl, but neither of us can be so precise about our purpose in life. Does that stop us from asking? I hope not, for these are the questions that bring meaning to life. Of them all, the most important is the first: Why are we here?

In this chapter and those that follow you will find questions that offer insights into why you are here. You will find stories and strategies to help you find answers. Presented in the form of seven steps to finding your purpose in life, these questions are the framework on which this book is built. They probe the musings of the head and the longings of the heart. "The heart has its reasons," wrote Pascal, "that reason can not know." It is with these that we start.

Yearnings

Life begins with desire. Nothing happens until there is yearning—for motion, for food, for connection, for change. Creation doesn't happen without desire; reproduction doesn't happen. The great accomplishments in the world do not merely happen, nor do the small events of day-to-day living.

The first yearning is for survival, for making it through this day and the next. Once this need is satisfied, according to psychologist Abraham Maslow, we want security—to know we are going to make it through the month. Next comes the need for human contact, to belong to and be accepted by people, to have meaningful relationships with those around us. Then come esteem needs, the longing to be respected for what we do. And finally the need for self-actualization, the urge to find our purpose in life . . . and to fulfill it.

A good illustration of this hierarchy of needs is the cave man who meets his survival needs by killing a buffalo and his security needs by smoking some of it to last through the winter. He meets his social needs by inviting the neighbors over for a buffalo banquet, and he meets his esteem needs by serving up barbecued buffalo to rave reviews. Then he finds a blank space on the wall of his cave and paints a picture of the whole adventure, satisfying his need for self-actualization by making sense of it all, for himself and others.

The purpose of this book is to get the painting up on the

wall. Everything leading to that act is important, in the life of the cave man or in our lives today, because it all arises from the basic yearnings of human existence. Those desires are where our search for purpose in life begins, with the first of seven steps.

Step One: What Do I Yearn For? What are the yearnings of my heart, the longings of my soul? Which are most important to me?

You may think of answers as you read the question, vague intuitions at the edge of memory, inklings of lost dreams, fragments of forgotten hopes. Write down what you know of your yearnings and then consider the following story about the power of dreams.

"In 1942 the destruction had already begun in Berlin," the CEO began. "Bread was hard to get and certain medicines could not be found. And yet people got married and had babies and 13-year-old girls like me had dreams. That spring I read *The German Merchant Abroad* and I said to my father, 'Papa, I want to be one of those,' and he said, 'My child, don't you realize, all of the people in that book are men,' and I said, 'I want to show the world that not all Germans are bad. Not all Germans are like Adolf Hitler.' "

She paused. "A couple of years ago I remembered that conversation and realized, My God, this is what I am doing!"

You probably had conversations like that when you were 13 or 11 or 15, longings that shape your life today. You had dreams, and they are worth remembering and recording. One way is to write WHAT DO I LONG FOR? and tape the note over your mirror. You can meditate on it, discuss it with a friend. Or you can try one or more of these three explorations, all of which have worked for participants in my workshops:

1. **Describe a perfect day in your life as you would like it to be two years from now.** Where do you wake up? With whom? How do you dress for your day? Who do you see? What activities engage your energies? Where do you have

lunch? With whom? How do you spend your afternoon? What is the end of your day like? With whom do you spend it? How do you feel as you review this day in the last moments before you fall asleep? You can do this as a meditation, as participants in my workshops often do, to get more inspired insights. You can write it down, you can illustrate it, you can add to it whenever you want.

2. **Draw a picture of your perfect life.** Use a large sheet of paper, as large as you can find. Use bright-colored markers and pastels. Use stickers. Use pictures cut from magazines or the newspaper. Use cartoons. Include both work and play in your picture—and friends and lovers, classes, travel, places to live and work, cars, trucks, and sailboats. Add labels and descriptive phrases to help capture your vision. Be adventurous, take some risks: this is not a test of your artistic ability but of your imagination. Show your vision to friends and notice how they react.

3. **Write a dialogue between your head and your heart.** Create a screenplay in which your head and your heart discuss their experience, their struggles, their longings. Use rational language for the head, passionate words for the heart. Avoid abstractions in favor of feelings, because these are most true. For realism, include a description of the setting and players and then create your dialogue, with head and heart alternating from the start and on to the conclusion of your choice. Here's how a young client of mine did this:

    Head: I want to make LOTS of money.
    Heart: What about my longing to paint?
    Head: Art can come later, when we can afford it.
    Heart: But our life will be barren without time to put oil on canvas.
    Head: How about a job as art director at a small ad agency, where our passion for color and form would pay off?
    Heart: Good thinking!

You can do all three of these explorations in less than an hour, or you can go for more detail and take longer. You can add to any of them as you get new thoughts, which inevitably will come. You can include other people in each of these three, by telling them what you have discovered, by showing them your work, by inviting them to participate.

Respect your yearnings. All of us have been told that we cannot have what we want—by our parents, by our teachers, by the Internal Revenue Service. "You don't deserve it," the life-denying voice repeats in our ear, the voice we must ignore if we are to find our purpose. Our desires and passions are hidden under years of denial, under a thousand "oughts" and "shoulds," which is why the first of the seven steps is the hardest—and the most fruitful.

Yearnings change, too, as we pass through the seasons of our lives. The romantic fantasies of our teenage years give way to riper dreams in middle life. If we stay with the game, confusion gives way to clarity, foolishness becomes wisdom—especially if we keep asking the questions and listen to even the most muted answers.

Heroic Clues

The second step to finding your purpose in life is to think of all the people you ever admired, respected, looked up to, or idolized.

Step Two: Whom Do I Find Heroic? What men and women from my own life and from the world around me do I most admire?

Here are three ways to delve into this question:

1. **Make a list of the heroes and heroines** from your family, including grandparents, aunts, nephews, and people you have never even met. Then think of people in sports, the arts, politics, religion, and school. Consider your neighbor-

hood and the world at large. Consider this time but also earlier times. Free associate, like the man who wrote, "Beethoven was gifted, as were Rembrandt and Ben Hogan." When you have as many names as you can come up with, note beside each what you admire about that person. One woman wrote, "Mother Teresa—because of her total dedication; Helen Keller—because of how she overcame adversity."

2. **Make a list of your antiheroes.** Who do you find repulsive and unbearable? To build your list, go through the same categories you used for heroic figures. Who do you hate as much as the young Berliner hated Adolf Hitler?

3. **Create your own hero or heroine.** Create your ideal person, using both positive and negative features. You can do this in words, with lists, or as a picture on a large sheet that could include images you cut from magazines. Either way, get as many attributes as you possibly can and then mark the three most important. One workshop participant wrote, "I would like to be many things I can't be and many things I possibly could be"—and then was surprised by how few characteristics were in the first category and how many in the second.

When you have finished this exercise, ask yourself what it tells you about your life. What inklings have you had about what is important and what is not? What clues have you found about your purpose in life? What are you learning that will help you shape your future like Jill Peel, whose words opened this chapter, sculpting them as a sculptor shapes clay?

If all this seems difficult, take heart: it is. Discovering purpose in life takes time, experience, and patience—as we are reminded by these words from Frederick Buechner in *The Sacred Journey:*

Through the alphabet of our years it takes many spellings out before we start to glimpse, or think we do, a little of what meaning is. Even then we glimpse it only dimly, like the first trace of dawn on the rim of night, and even then it is a meaning that we cannot fix and be sure of once and for all because it is always incarnate meaning and thus as alive and changing as we are ourselves alive and changing.

So push on, persevere, continue the search for meaning and purpose in your life. It is worth the effort.

3

Learning Success

I am always ready to learn, but I do not always like being taught.

—Winston Churchill

The ability to learn faster than your competitors is the only sustainable competitive advantage.

—Arie De Geus, director, Royal Dutch/Shell

"My biggest client is about to fire me," the company president was saying. "They account for 30 percent of my business, over $3 million a year."

What had led to this calamity?

"We supply temporary clerical personnel for their main office, including the mail room. The last three mail clerks we sent over have all been duds. The first couldn't read, the second disappeared into the men's room on the second day and was never seen again. The third opened a box of VISA cards intended for their executives and was found four days later at the Hilton Hotel in Montreal. He ran up $3,600 on the cards before he was arrested, and the charges are still coming in.

"We have an excellent record overall—nobody works as hard as we do to find good temps and nobody screens them as carefully. But this client has its temp business out for bid right now and one of the three people on the committee reviewing the bids is the mail room supervisor, who is furious with us.

"What should I do?"

Use my sense of humor, she decided, and my imagination. After living with the problem for an hour she decided to send the angry mail room supervisor a box of lemons. She sent her assistant to the corner produce stand to make the purchase and before gift wrapping and delivering it to her client, she added this card:

> **Please enjoy these because they are the last lemons you will be getting from us.**

Two weeks later came the good news: her company was once again chosen as the supplier of temporary personnel for this client. Besides that, they want her to bid on a major piece of new business.

Did the lemons help? Probably. It also helped that the president has built a company with an excellent reputation for top-quality people. She has figured out how to use her talent and passion to achieve her goals. She has learned success by using this strategy, one of many you will find as you continue through this book:

Success Strategy: Heed history. Identify the good parts in your past and put more of them in your future. Reverse the old adage—Those who fail to understand history are condemned to repeat it—by using your personal history to make life better.

This is also expressed as the third step to finding your purpose in life:

Step Three: How Am I Successful? How have I faced adversity and achieved my desires? What do the transcendent experiences and times of fulfillment in my life tell me about my future?

Why focus on success? Failure may teach us more, but success is a better reflection of our motivation, effort, and ability. It is a reflection of where our talent is directed—and where the universe conspires in our favor. Small successes, especially those born of failure, are as important as large ones. Early successes are as important as recent ones.

In considering Step Three, the woman who sent lemons to her unhappy client remembers these successes:

- When she was in eighth grade, one of her watercolors won top prize in an art show in the small Oregon town where she grew up.
- At UCLA she was elected vice-president of the sophomore class after running a dorm room to dorm room campaign.
- Laid off by a major personnel firm, she started her own company, now one of the best in the West, with $9,000.
- Married in her mid-thirties, she and her entrepreneur husband are raising two healthy children. "I don't really see this as 'success,'" she told me later. "My family is a great source of joy, everything I ever dreamed of."

You too can learn from your achievements, especially if you break success into three parts and try these tools:

1. **Consider past successes,** using one or more of these three approaches:
   - Draw your life line. Use the longest piece of paper you can find, starting at the beginning of your life and ending with today. Unless you are like the lawyer at one of my talks who drew his line perfectly straight except for a dip when he got a B in fifth grade, you will start to see a pattern, a picture of your past. The peaks in your line— and *almost* all of us have peaks and valleys—are where success lies. Once you have drawn the line, from birth to right now, label the important points with dates and descriptive phrases. Highlight your successes.
   - Create a chronology of life activities, starting with school projects and early jobs. Date each activity and describe

what you did, listing several accomplishments for each job. When you are through, check your file of old résumés to see if you have missed anything. Then go back with a highlighter and mark your successes.

• Write an obituary for yourself, as it would appear if you got hit by a truck tomorrow. Make it as long and detailed as you can. Tell stories, like the lemon story that opened this chapter, to illustrate your life. Add everything you can think of and then go back with a highlighter and mark the successes. When you are finished, make a photocopy of this story to save for your grandchildren.

2. **Present success.** Make a list of successes in your life today. Include small ones like "operating within budget" or "building new relationships." Include big ones that are in the middle of happening or just beginning. Evaluate your life, focusing on the positive. Take your time. Capture every success you can think of. You are looking for patterns here, as well as ideas.

3. **Future successes.** Go back to step one and think about what successes would fulfill your longings. What do you need to achieve to have your perfect day two years from now? What needs to happen for the picture of your life to be perfect? What successes will bring your head and your heart into harmony? Your list of future successes is the most important, because it rises from the richness of your past and the poignancy of your present. Highlight the most important items on your list and put a star beside the three you care most deeply about.

The fourth step to finding your purpose in life flows directly from the third, because the successes we have and aspire to grow out of our enthusiasms.

Step Four: What Are My Enthusiasms? What values, beliefs, and life issues are most important to me? What do I care about most? What inspires me? Where does my passion lie?

As with success, the perspective of time helps us understand our enthusiasms. How they evolve from the childhood days of heavy parental influence to adult independence is part of what we want to learn.

1. Enthusiasms from growing up. What values and beliefs shaped your early years? Make a list of influential people in your early life and note what you learned from each. Were there important teachers? A priest or rabbi? A coach or mentor? Write down as many as you can think of. Note what they contributed to your worldview and highlight the important words. "I can't remember any values growing up," a 52-year-old man said recently in one of my seminars. What about your father? After a long pause, we saw that he was on the verge of tears. "My father always said, 'You can do anything you want to do.' " He blew his nose and said, "That still shapes my life today."

2. Enthusiasms from your life today. These reflect your experience in getting here. What are you doing that excites you? Makes you feel good? That you tell people about? That you want to do more of tomorrow? Look at these activities and see what values and beliefs they represent. The words I hear most often are: honesty, integrity, nurturing, "The Golden Rule," learning, service, excellence, achievement, loyalty, family. Write your own words in a column and highlight the most important.

3. Enthusiasms you expect to shape your future. What kind of person do you want to be? What words would you like others to use in describing the future you? How might your children talk about you? When the time comes to sum up your life, what will be the main themes? If someone was writing a book about your life, what would the title be? The subtitle? When you have this down, highlight the words that are most important to you. What does this tell you about purpose in your life?

In a recent workshop, Bill talked about his successes as a schoolteacher, about the learning environments he had created, and about the young people who had discovered the joy of education in his classroom. Bill values "the worthy cause of truth" and though he is retired now, he wants to make education better. "I could spend the rest of my days in that endeavor," he told the group as he described plans to volunteer for work in a local public school.

As you contemplate your successes and enthusiasms, let Bill's example inspire you. "The worthy cause of truth" is not an easy one, especially when we are looking for answers to life's most profound questions. But truth does emerge, one piece at a time, if we continue the search.

The search continues for the company president who kept her biggest customer with an unusual gift. Her sense of humor, her determination, and the high value she places on excellence combined to create success for her—and will do so again. As with you and me, her successes reflect her enthusiasms.

Along the way, lemons may come into your life—in the form of dishonest people, unexpected disasters, or plans that collapse. There's not much help for that. It happens to all of us. But all of us can choose what to do with the lemons in our lives. We can put them in a box, add a ribbon, and send them off with a smile. Or we can cut them up, give them a squeeze, and invite friends in for a glass of lemonade.

CHAPTER

4

Friends and Purpose

If thou seest a man of understanding, get
thee betimes unto him, and let thy foot
wear the steps of his door.

—Ecclesiastes 6:36

The inner king is the one in us who knows
what we want to do for the rest of our
lives, or the rest of the month, or the rest
of the day. He can make clear what we
want without being contaminated in his
choice by the opinions of others around
us. The inner king is connected with our
fire of purpose and passion.

—Robert Bly, *Iron John*

"Sheer ignorance," says Margot Fraser. "That's how I got into business. I didn't read a book at first, which was lucky, because it would have paralyzed me."

While vacationing in Germany in 1966, Fraser bought a pair of Birkenstock sandals and liked them so much she began ordering small quantities for friends. At a 1968 health food convention, where Fraser had rented a small booth, she remembers a woman who arrived on sore feet and departed in ecstasy. "She bought four pairs, all in her size, and went on to launch the first successful retail operation for Birkenstock in this country."

Fraser almost gave up on Birkenstocks in 1970 when she was divorced from her first husband, an importer. But people kept asking her about those comfortable sandals and so she called

Karl Birkenstock in Germany. How would he feel about doing business with a woman? "Absolutely fine!"

There are no accidents, in life or in business. Nothing happens, good or bad, that does not fit some cosmic plan. We may not see it at the time, but every daily encounter with our environment, with those around us, with our own humanity, has significance in our lives. Every meeting, at the health food show or on the street this afternoon, has a purpose, however small and obscure.

Margot Fraser is one of those entrepreneurs who stumble into success—on purpose. "Human beings are extremely adaptable," she once told me. "We don't know what's in us until it's called for." Fraser did not set out to become the leader of a remarkable company. Her early training as a seamstress and dress designer gave her no clue that she would create the North American distribution company for Birkenstock sandals, providing employment for hundreds of people—and comfort for thousands.

Windows

The first four steps to finding your purpose in life invite you to consider yearnings, heroes, successes, and enthusiasms. When you understand these you are ready for the fifth step, which brings the first four into focus:

> **Step Five: Windows.** Look into your goals, ideals, skills, and interests for integrating ideas about your purpose.

Imagine that there are four windows through which you can peer into the deepest recesses of your inner world. You may see similar things through two windows, but each window is different and together they afford you a view of your mission in life.

Here are the four windows:

- **GOALS.** In this first window are the goals you hold most dear. These are the yearnings from Step One and the long-term objectives from your life plan. Looking through this window people often see "financial security" (or in one case, "massive wealth") or "family happiness" or "learning." Other goals might be "to become president" or "to work on Wall Street." How about you? What are your goals?

- **IDEALS.** In the second window you see your values, attitudes, and beliefs—your enthusiasms, what you care about. These may be big ideals like "the worthy cause of truth" or "protecting the environment" or even "happiness." I encourage you to be precise when looking through this window, asking yourself, for instance, if happiness is an ideal for me, what makes me happy? Be specific, like the business leader whose painting has taught her that she values beauty, symmetry, color, order, and passion.

- **WAYS, SKILLS, TALENTS.** Through the third window you see what you are good at, the ways you operate at your best, the unique competencies you use in achieving what you care about. As you look through this window, you should think of action words like leading, persuading, negotiating, building, connecting, teaching, coaching. Be specific. HOW do you lead? HOW do you persuade? Look back at Step Three and see what you did to achieve your successes. One of the most effective people I know considers himself a "pioneer." How about you? What is your key word?

- **FIELDS.** The fourth window gives a view of where you do what you're good at. It's the meadow in which you play. It's what career you pick or what business you go into. It's what people mean when they ask professors, "What is your field?" Clients of mine have pursued their purpose in jewelry design, computing, healing, house building. You can play in a bigger field, too, like my friend the pioneer, whose field is "information technology."

If you take a sheet of paper and draw four windows on it, like those below, you will get a clearer picture of your mission. What purpose emerges from the words you write in these windows?

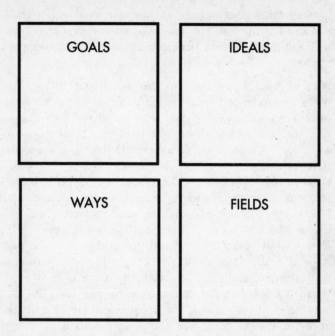

Here is a way to make Step Five work for you:

> **Success Strategy:** Try purposes on for size. See how they feel.
> Walk around with them for a few days. Modify and shape them
> until they get comfortable. Test different words and phrases. See
> how they sound. Look at them on paper. Our life direction does
> not change much over time, but the way we express it can get
> more colorful, more precise, more powerful.

You can try out your ideas on friends, too, which is the sixth
step:

> **Step Six: Friends.** Ask at least five friends—more is better—
> how they see your purpose in life.

This step takes your search for purpose to a higher level. You are no longer flying solo, as you were on the first five steps, and feedback will give you new perspective. Here are some guidelines:

- **Who to Ask.** If you live with someone, start there. You can try your circle of friends, people at work, people you play with. Try your coaches, counselors, and mentors. Some people, you will notice, have not paid much attention to you and won't be able to offer help. Others will respond with rich reflection.
- **What to Ask.** You can ask directly about purpose, but less direct questions usually work better. "As you see me, what am I best at?" "In your experience, what motivates me?" "From where you see it, what do I care more about?" Tell your friend what you have learned going through the first five steps and ask, "Does that seem right to you?" "What would you add or change?" "Can you say more?"
- **What to Look For.** Be on the alert for words or phrases you may have missed. Look for unique and precise words that apply to you alone. Look for people who have a sense of purpose you can link to, bounce off, settle down beside. Look for fresh ideas. Look for surprises.

Paul Wingate was in a workshop I led recently on "Men, Meaning, and Work." In the final meeting, after going through these steps, Paul talked with the group about purpose. "I love building homes," he told us, "that are light and cozy, with no sharp corners and no toxics." He explained the dangers of arsenic salts in pressure-treated wood and he told us of his passion for creating living spaces that are good for people. He listened to our ideas. At the end we agreed with him when he said, "My purpose in life is building healthy homes."

If you are still not sure of your purpose, try Step Seven:

Step Seven: Inspiration. Listen to your intuition, inner voices, spiritual sources. Ask: Why am I here?

The inspiration you find may be a creative breakthrough, an "Aha! That's it!" It may be inspiration in the theological sense, "Divine guidance exerted directly on the mind and soul," or it may come from what Robert Bly calls the inner king. It will almost certainly involve breathing in, which is the meaning of the Latin root word *inspirare*.

When I take CEO groups or workshop participants through this step, I use words like those that follow. You can use similar words, perhaps accompanied by music, read to you by a friend or recorded by you and played back. Notice where these words take you:

Find a comfortable position, with your back straight. Take a deep breath, exhale, and close your eyes. Take another deep breath, exhale, and go in your mind's eye to a special place, your very own special place, by the beach, in the mountains, in a meadow—whatever feels best to you. Look around. Notice the colors and shapes. Smell the air. Now lean over and pick up a small object you will see by your right foot. Examine it, smell it. Look up. You will see a figure approaching. This is your all-knowing, all-seeing friend. Notice how your friend walks. Notice what your friend is wearing. When your friend is close enough, make eye contact. Greet your friend with a hand clasp or an embrace. Tell your friend that you have three questions and then ask, "What work is right for me? What is the best use of my talent, knowledge, passion?" . . . Ask again. Ask for specifics . . . "What work is right for me?" . . . Sometimes the last answer is the best one . . . When you are satisfied, ask a second question: "Why was I put here? What is my purpose on this planet?" . . . Ask again. Listen for specifics. "What is my purpose in life?" . . . When you are satisfied, ask a third question of your own choosing. Ask a private question of your all-knowing, all-seeing friend and see what you hear. . . . Listen closely, because the last part may be the best. . . . Now see if your friend is willing to meet with you again. If you intend to do this, tell your friend. Now bid farewell to your friend, with a hand clasp or an embrace. Make eye contact. Watch your friend depart. How do you feel? . . . Now look again at the object in your right hand. Notice how it has become more vivid. Put it on the ground again by your right foot. Look around your special place. Notice details, colors, shapes, smells, and resolve to remember them. When you are ready, take a deep breath. Exhale. Now another, and come back into this place and this time and open your eyes.

Once people start to stir I ask them to write down their experience and insights. I encourage you to do the same. You might get original wisdom. You might get confirmation of what you already know. You might not get much at all. Not to worry: This kind of intuitive exercise gets better with practice. My respect for it went up sharply when I asked my all-knowing, all-seeing friend this third question: "Will I make a difference in the world?" Quick as a flash came the answer, "Yes, but not much."

Whew! What a relief, I thought, when I finished laughing. It's not all on my shoulders. Nor is it all on yours. But all of us benefit ourselves and others by becoming clearer on purpose. Especially when we do it together, with friends and others, because collective action calls up extra energy. I saw this in a meeting room recently overlooking the Pacific Ocean when 18 people put their personal mission statements—words, colors, images, pictures—on the windows, backlit by the sun setting over the sea. They were stating their purposes using the steps described in these first four chapters. Eighteen people expressing their intent and supporting one another, their spirit flooding the room. If you want meaning, look for friends like this. Find new ways to align with others. Let your lives together make a difference.

PART

II

Stages of the Career Cycle

5

Heroic Journeys

In the middle of the journey of our life I
came to myself in a dark wood where the
straight way was lost.

—Dante, *Inferno*

There is a typical hero sequence of actions
which can be detected from all over the
world and from many, many periods of
history. It is essentially one deed done by
many different people.

—Joseph Campbell

Reality is made up of circles, but we see in
straight lines.

—Peter Senge, *The Fifth Discipline*

Hero was beautiful, according to artists of old, and her love for
Leander is legendary. Hero served Aphrodite, the Greek goddess
of love, as a priestess, and trysted nightly in her tower at Sestos
with Leander, who swam the Hellespont from Abydos for every
assignation, drawn by the force of his love and by a light set in
the tower by his lover.

One stormy night the wind blew out the flame and Leander
lost his way, was overwhelmed by the waves, and drowned. At
dawn, an anxious Hero discovered his body floating beneath the
tower. In her grief the young priestess leaped into the sea and
herself was drowned.

While Hero's name is now used to describe courageous males,

her exploits belong to all of us. The joy of her love and the pain of her loss are part of what every man or woman encounters on the heroic journey.

The Trip

If you did the life-line exercise in Chapter 3 you know that it's not hard to see life as linear. In this rational age we are taught to think that way, to visualize life on a graph that begins at birth and heads off toward death. We imagine our life progress will be like the sales line for Apple or Microsoft—always tending upward, with a blip here or there.

The problem with a linear view is that it starts out of a void and ends in a void. It gives us meager aid in understanding our future and offers scant comfort on downturns. It diminishes hope. It limits possibilities. The linear view promotes competition, as in "My earnings line is higher than yours" or "My net worth is bigger than yours."

These difficulties troubled me as I prepared to lead a workshop on "Life Change, Career Change" in March of 1981. Pacing the room, 10 minutes before meeting the group, I discovered a sheet, left by some earlier occupant, featuring a large circle representing "The Hero's Journey." It was on the front page of an article by Paul Rebillot, based on Joseph Campbell's model from *The Hero with a Thousand Faces*, which I had read years earlier and forgotten.

Bingo! This is it, I realized. This is a way to make sense of the ups and downs of my 14 years in business. This is how I can explain the renewal I'm feeling in my professorial career. This is the way to help those on the down slope see that there is hope, there is better to come, there is a path, there is purpose.

What could be more natural than a circle? Up and down lines, with distinct beginnings and endings, are rare in the natural world. But everywhere on our planet there are circles, cycles, and spheres.

The pebble dropped in a pond creates concentric circles, growing larger. Man's earliest invention, the wheel, is a circle in motion. The full (circle) moon in the night sky comes every

28 days, and we now know this is because the moon rotates in a circular orbit around the earth. This planet is a sphere—a three-dimensional circle—spinning in a circular orbit that produces night and day. This circular orbit around the sun produces the seasons and is the most common pattern in our solar system and in the universe.

Why not look at life as a recurring, circular pattern? A rhythm where downs are followed by ups and where the future is predictable, like the seasons? Why not see life as a series of cycles rather than a lonely, linear experience? Eastern religions teach reincarnation—a recurring cycle of life—and many myths suggest a circular journey.

A typical hero sequence in myth involves a journey downward and a return trip, often perilous, before coming home. As Joseph Campbell saw, this cycle is rich in meaning. If you and I want to know more about our purpose in life, there is much we can learn from the heroic exploits of mythic travelers on this path. Here are examples from three stories.

Getting Seduced

Life journeys, then and now, begin in response to inner urges. We may set off seeking happiness, success, victory, love. Sometimes we are fleeing failure and unhappiness. Usually we are attracted by what we hope lies ahead.

When Odysseus, king of Ithaca, says good-bye to his wife Penelope and goes to fight in the Trojan War, it is because he has been recruited to the Greek cause by Agamemnon. In the Homeric epic poem, written some 2700 years ago, Odysseus is victorious in battle but has difficulty with the journey home:

- Odysseus and his men get blown off course on the return voyage and end up prisoners on the island of Ogygia, where the sea nymph Calypso takes Odysseus "for her bed-mate." Like many of us, this hero is seduced early in the voyage. And like many of us, he is well seduced: it takes seven years for Odysseus to escape from Calypso's island.

- Leaving Ogygia, Odysseus and his men are beset by a storm that destroys their ship. Staggering ashore on the island of the Phaecians, our hero is discovered by the king's daughter, who hopes that this man "might settle contentedly in our city and agree to be called my husband." Despite the fact that he's already married, the young maiden takes him off to her palace.
- At the palace, Odysseus tells of yet another island, where his men are turned into pigs by the enchantress Circe, who then makes their leader her lover. "Let us two go lie together," says Circe, "that we may mingle our bodies and learn to trust one another." Poor Odysseus is seduced again.

But Circe holds the key to his liberation, because she tells Odysseus that in order to get home he must visit the underworld, where the prophet Teiresias will show him the way home to Ithaca. Down he goes, to the land of the dead, and then back to Circe, who warns Odysseus about the Sirens, sea nymphs whose beautiful singing lures seamen to their death.

Wiser now from his experiences of love on the journey, Odysseus has himself tied to the mast so he cannot respond to the seductive call of the Sirens. He has learned to resist. He is ready to return to Ithaca, after 10 years of venturing, to rejoin his faithful, long-loving wife.

Like Odysseus, you and I face seduction on our life voyage—the temptations of power, money, fame, and the easy life sung out by society. Like Odysseus, we must learn to resist or die. We learn to discriminate, to make choices that move us along on the path, but the lessons almost always come from surrendering to temptation.

Those who head businesses understand such temptations, as I was reminded recently in telling a group of Seattle CEOs about Odysseus. They smiled at his plight and one even laughed. "That guy," she said, "sounds just like my ex-husband."

Getting Undressed

Seduction invites us to burn through our desires, to abandon old compulsions and worn identities, to shuck them off like unneeded garments. On one level, this is the story of Inanna, "Queen of Heaven, of the place where the sun rises."

In this 5000-year-old Sumerian myth, Inanna decides to go to the underworld. "Abandoned heaven, abandoned earth," says the poem, "to the Netherworld she descended." When Erishkegal, Queen of the Great Below, learns of this intruder, she insists that Inanna, like anyone entering this kingdom, be brought "naked and bowed low."

At each of the seven gates to the "land of no return" a gatekeeper removes one piece of Inanna's queenly regalia until she is "crouched and stripped bare." Then, the myth tells us, Inanna is killed by Erishkegal.

Inanna's downward journey mirrors our own passage through the great cycle of life. The peeling away of excess garments happens to us just as it happened to Inanna, as we give up unneeded or unhelpful attitudes and beliefs. If we travel this great cycle, we must leave behind illusions:

- The illusion of CONTROL, as we face forces larger than ourselves
- The illusion of UNIQUENESS, as we sink into the universal
- The illusion of SUPERIORITY, as we are humbled
- The illusion of INFERIORITY, as we accept ourselves
- The illusion of SEPARATENESS, as we join with others in celebrating our humanness
- The illusion of INVINCIBILITY, as we encounter disappointment, defeat, despair
- The illusion of IMMORTALITY, as we face death at the bottom of the cycle.

At the bottom Inanna is revived when two mourners bring her the food and water of life. Returning home through the seven gates, she reclaims her vestments, in much the same way that we reclaim the illusions that color our lives. These psychic garments are different, though, on the return trip—however similar to those left behind, these are worn more lightly.

Homecoming

A third ancient story illustrates a final point about the circular journeys of life: no matter how hard the hard parts and how low the low spots there is a reward at the end. There is a blessing, a gift, something to share with the world, what Joseph Campbell called a "boon." Nowhere is this reward seen more powerfully than in the biblical story of Job.

"There was a man in the land of Uz," the story begins, with seven sons and three daughters, "seven thousand sheep and three thousand camels and five hundred yoke of oxen." And Job was "the greatest of all the men of the east."

All this soon changes, as Job starts his journey. His children are killed, his livestock stolen, and even his health is taken away, as the devil inflicts Job "with sore boils from the sole of his foot unto his crown." When things go bad, they all go bad, as many of us have discovered firsthand.

At the bottom, Job becomes "a brother to dragons and a companion to owls" but as he emerges from misery he is told to "deck thyself now with majesty and excellency." Job responds, "I have heard of thee by the hearing of the ear: but now mine eyes seeth thee." Job has new powers of perception. Out of his pain comes wisdom and a clear view of life.

Just in case the listener isn't convinced that Job has been improved by his ordeal, the story says that his children are restored to him and also his livestock, which are now 14,000 sheep, 6,000 camels, and 1,000 yoke of oxen—enough to satisfy even the most materialistic, then or now.

"So the Lord blessed the latter end of Job more than the beginning." Job completed the cycle in a better place, as though his life were an ascending spiral, a helix. For us too there are rewards for completing each cycle, boons and blessings to enhance our lives and the lives of those we love.

Travelers Today

As Joseph Campbell liked to say, we can all take the heroic journey. Like Odysseus, Inanna, or Job, we go down in order to come up. No two journeys are identical. Parts of the adventure may be longer for one person than for another and events may come in unexpected sequences, but each trip is part of a universal pattern.

After years spent studying hundreds of career cycles—in books, in workshops, in counseling sessions—I see seven stages in this heroic journey. While my focus has been on careers, notice how these stages also describe cycles of love and cycles of life.

- *Discontent* is the itch that gets us started. It is a call to adventure, like the one heard by Odysseus, Inanna, and Job—and it usually proves irresistible. On the career cycle it can be a bad stretch or boredom at work, a difficult boss, or a pink slip. However it comes, the call must be heeded.
- *Exploring* is the healthy response to discontent. It starts with inner exploration, with the search for self-knowledge, and grows into the development of options out in the world. Experienced travelers continue to explore wherever they are on the cycle.
- *Committing* happens when enough exploring has been done. It is the "yes" that supercedes "maybe." It is the decision in the face of risk—to take a new assignment, to take a new job, to change careers. Commitment empowers us through the bottom of the cycle.
- *Changing* comes at the bottom of the cycle, as we plunge into the underworld and the dark night of the soul. Change can be tumultuous, especially change in our work lives, but it is always a time of heightened learning. Transformation is never easy, and inner transformation—which is at the heart of career change—is most difficult of all.
- *Renewal* is the exuberant rebirth as we emerge from the bottom of the cycle. It is the joy of escape and the delight in

new powers. It is enthusiasm and high energy for fresh challenges. It is the happy time when the storm is over.

- *Integrating* is when we are heading home to our familiar foibles and human frailties. If, like me, you have always had trouble with numbers, you will still have trouble with numbers, no matter how much you have learned this time around.
- *Recommitting* to another trip is the last stage in the cycle. Recommitment may be conscious or it may just happen, but almost everyone goes around more than once. Recommitment becomes easy when we are empowered by purpose in our lives.

Putting these stages together, the cycle looks like this:

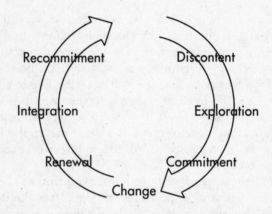

When we see our life as a cycle, with recurring patterns, the changes make sense. We understand where we have been and we live more fully at the stage we are in because we have some idea of where we are going. We can find ourselves on the map, which is a comforting experience. We know the path of purpose, the journey of life discovery.

"This map sure fits my life," said a CEO who heard these stages described, "and I wish it didn't. I'm exploring right now because my business is awful and my partner is worse. I know things have got to change—I'm approaching commitment—and it's not going to be fun. This map is helpful, though, because at least now I know where I'm going."

"So these are career cycles?" another says, smiling. "These changes I've been going through for so many years are cycles? And here all this time I thought I was just going around in circles!"

Success Strategy: Use ancient heroic figures to empower your life. What can you learn from Odysseus, Inanna, and Job? What would these mythic heroes do if encountering your problems? How would they advise you? Make allies of Odysseus, Inanna, Job, and other totemic figures who attract you. Their stories linger because their lives have much to teach.

CHAPTER

6

Divine Discontent

To be discontented with the divine
discontent, and to be ashamed with the
noble shame, is the very germ and first
upgrowth of all virtue.

—Charles Kingsley, *Health and Education*, 1874

A purpose is not the same as wanting to
be rich. Or wanting to control the junk
bond market. Or wanting to be dominant
over other men in the business world. Or
to have many mistresses. We ask men to
become dissatisfied with their lives.

—Robert Bly, to interviewer

How can your sales manager be burned
out if he's never been on fire?

—Donald Sullivan, furniture company
president

"My passion is gone, dead, nowhere," Bruce told the circle of
men. "No fire, no desire."

As we listened Bruce described all that he had done in his 36
years. "I've been a carpenter, a stone mason, a builder of houses.
I've been a platform diver, a deep-sea diver, a sky diver. I have a
contractor's license and a private pilot's license. Nothing appeals
anymore."

Several men had ideas for Bruce about sparking his next career, and he seemed less shrunk down inside himself and more

confident by the end of the evening. But it was clear that there would be more discontent for Bruce before he found joy.

Pleasure is what all of us seek, in love and work, but there is always pain along the path. Without pain, there is no pleasure. What keeps us moving, what keeps the search active, is discontent, the gnawing unhappiness of being in one job too long or the sharp pain of a new assignment gone sour.

Discontent has a thousand faces. It can be barely noticeable or it can be intense. It can be a little bit once in a while or it can be all-engulfing and all-the-time. A progressive form of discontent is burnout, "a syndrome of emotional exhaustion, depersonalization, and reduced personal accomplishment," according to Christina Maslach's book on the subject. Burnout is too much giving and not enough receiving, too much emotional outflow with not enough psychic nourishing. Energy reserves become depleted, resistance to illness lowered; there is inefficiency, dissatisfaction, and pessimism.

Whether discontent comes from burnout or a termination notice or a mismatch at work, the question each of us has to ask, sooner or later, is: What is going to light my fire?

The Call

Discontent is the call to adventure for the hero or heroine about to start on the great journey. It is a beckoning signal ignored at great peril. It is a distant glimmer that draws us, if we are willing to respond, closer and closer to the flame. It is the Netherworld that draws Inanna, the battle that calls Odysseus.

This call can be barely heard or it can be like a trumpet blast. Sometimes barely seen, it also can be a blinding flash. See how it works in these four stories about actual people.

Jean is a therapist, a good one, and quite happy now that she has confronted her discontent. She still remembers her anger at the professional in the office next to hers, a man who was barely civil and often neglected to give her messages from clients. "The worst was when he told a young woman waiting in my outer office that I was a lesbian," Jean recalls. "I was furious!" Confronting her neighbor was like talking to a potato, Jean found, so she took a scary step and signed a lease for new space. A year later, she is delighted with the change. "It's a bigger office, with neighbors I love, and the growth in my practice has way more than covered the cost of the move."

Gail is a sociology instructor and published author who earned her Ph.D. at Cornell. When she came up for promotion to associate professor, Gail was excited—her student evaluations were excellent, her committee work was sound, and her research papers were being published in major journals. She was sure her application would succeed, but the faculty review committee thought otherwise, and Gail was crushed. "I almost quit, but then I decided to test the water first and signed on to teach a section of Introductory Sociology at the state university across town, where I was pretty sure I could get a full-time appointment if I wanted it." The politics were even worse there than where she had been teaching, Gail discovered, and she would have to share both an office and a parking space. Her reaction? "I stuck it out and the next year I got my promotion at Cornell with rave reviews. I know I made the right decision."

Tom works for a contractor repairing earthquake damage in San Francisco and finishing walls in luxury homes. Although earning more money than most of those with whom he graduated from college a year ago, he is feeling burned out. "I worked 60 hours last week," he laments, "and that doesn't include some horrendous commutes. There's paint and dirt and dust in all my clothes and in my car, and my boss owes me $1,200." How is Tom dealing with his discontent? He is studying for his California real estate sales license and talking to local firms about commercial real estate sales positions. Progress is slow, because he's still doing construction work, but he's sure he will make the transition. "What I find in job interviews these days," he says, smiling, "is that I'm lots more motivated than I ever was before."

Bill built his company to $50 million in sales and then was summarily dismissed by the board of directors, tossed out

with only a fraction of what his stock had been worth just a
year earlier. What happened? "The bean counters were stran-
gling my company," is how Bill sees it. Others think Bill was
a free-spending visionary who neglected day-to-day management chores. Wherever the truth lies, Bill had been increas-
ingly unhappy at the company he and his wife started. "I
was shocked when the board suspended me," Bill reflects,
"but I was also relieved, like a huge burden had just been
taken off my shoulders." Because he's creative and entrepre-
neurial, Bill is now criss-crossing the country finding new
products to promote. "This is without a doubt the best thing
that could have happened," says Bill, who is confident that
his new life will be better than the one he is leaving behind.

Jean, Gail, and Tom all acted on their discontent. Even Bill,
who got moving when he got fired, was active in creating a better
work life for himself. All dealt with discontent in one of its many
forms, which look something like this:

Intensity of Discontent	Symptoms of Discontent	Cause of Discontent
Occasional	Lagging interest	Unappealing assignment
Mild	Doubts about work	Bad day
Light	Mild concerns	Grouchy boss
Frequent	Boredom	Conflict with boss
Gnawing	Bad dreams	Business turns sour
Annoying	Mild depression	Company acquired
Disconcerting	Weight gain	
	Weight loss	
	Lost enthusiasm	
All the time	Chronic depression	Demoted
Grinding	Back goes out	Layed off
Palpable	Ulcers	Forced to resign
Crippling	Sleeplessness	Fired for cause
Immobilizing	Nightmares	

We have all felt some form of discontent. For some of us the discontent has been intense, falling into several of the categories listed here. We have known times of less than total contentment and we all have the capacity to learn from the experience, to discover what we are being told about our purpose in life.

In my 10-year academic career, I tasted many kinds of discontent, starting with bland varieties that inspired me to work smarter and moving to more potent blends that ultimately led to my resignation. Now when I notice discontent in my life, I check its quality and ask myself if it is a signal to get moving. Is it time for a course correction? What action, however small, is called for?

Discontent can be uncomfortable, but we do not have to stay mired in it. Instead, it can mobilize us. Discontent is different for each of us but the end result, if the signals are heeded, is the same. What matters is that we embark on the heroic journey.

The Cycle

When asked about the heroic adventure, Joseph Campbell said:

> The usual hero adventure begins with someone from whom something has been taken, or who feels there's something lacking in the normal experiences available or permitted to the members of his society. This person then takes off on a series of adventures beyond the ordinary, either to recover what has been lost or to discover some life-giving elixir. It's usually a cycle, a going and a returning.

Discontent is like that. We feel as though something has been taken: the joy that comes from doing good work, the satisfaction of working with people we like, the fulfillment of being respected for our accomplishments. And if it hasn't been taken, if we have merely lost it or given it away or if we never had it to begin with, we notice the lack anyway, and feel the discontent with equal intensity.

The heroic response, Campbell tells us, is to take off, to leave the winter of our discontent for the summer sun further along the cycle. The question is when. Because however discontented we are, our malaise is heightened by a kind of cosmic impatience, arising from the knowledge that we will not be here forever.

Time the Master, Time the Servant

All great cycles occur in time. The planet on which we live takes 24 hours for a complete rotation. It takes 13 full moons for a full trip through the seasons. The other planets in our solar system have recurring time patterns for their cycles, and scientists say the same is true for every cycle in the universe.

Life is measured from sunrise to sunrise, from spring to spring, and by how often the moon comes up full. The span of a single lifetime, from first breath to last, can be measured by these natural cycles.

We cannot imagine the earth or the moon or the planets stopping in time, and yet our own lives, and especially our work lives, sometimes seem to come to a halt. When that happens, discontent is acute.

As John Steinbeck wrote in *Sweet Thursday:*

> Where does discontent start? You are warm enough but you shiver. You are fed, yet hunger gnaws you. You have been loved, but your yearning wanders in new fields. And to prod all these there's time, the Bastard Time.

The Bastard Time is merciless. It treats us all alike and if we do not feel right about our life it heightens our discomfort cruelly. If we are not to have fulfillment now, then when? If we are not to find satisfaction here, then where? How long must we be discontent?

To answer this question for yourself, try this exploration, one of several you will find in coming chapters:

> **Exploration: Where Is My Discontent Leading?** On a plain sheet of paper draw a line across the top and one down the middle, forming a T. Label the left-hand column "Discontent in my work life" and list sources of pain. Label the right-hand column "Action I will take" and for each item on the left write what you plan to do.

Here's how a client of mine did this exploration:

Where Is My Discontent Leading?

Discontent at work	Action I will take
• Meetings with boss too long	• Prepare agendas
• Subordinates given work by other managers	• Clarify lines of authority and let others know
• Too much to do	• Prioritize tasks
• Operations guy belittles me	• Talk straight with him, clarify our roles

Whether you are a frustrated middle manager like my client, an unhappy sky diver who has lost his passion, or a burned-out helping professional, there are things you can do to make your life better. How? Heed the call. Respond to the discontent.

Do not be misled into thinking that response is easy, however, because discontent can be subtle and fleeting, or it can be pervasive yet misunderstood. It can be divine or it can be common. It can be mild and it can be overpowering. But whatever its form, discontent calls for action. Whether the response is small or large, interior and attitudinal or expressed out in the world, ultimately the resolution for discontent lies in action.

My client spoke with the operations manager. "Things are better now," he reports. "There is a lot more respect. And meetings with my boss are half as long now that we use an agenda."

Make your discontent divine. Make it work for you and for

others, as my client did. Let it empower you. Let it start you to-day on the road to change. Remember the advice Dear Abby gave to "Feeling Low in Tacoma": "Don't despair. The world is round. What looks like the end may be only the beginning."

CHAPTER

7

Always Exploring

The journey of a thousand miles begins
with a single step.

—Lao-tzu

The best advice I ever heard was "There
are two questions a man must ask himself.
The first is 'Where am I going?' and the
second is 'Who will go with me?' "

—Sam Keen, *Fire in the Belly*

Of all the stages in the life cycle, none is more essential for successful living than exploration. Of all the skills we acquire on the Ferris wheel of life, the most rewarding are those that lead us to discovery.

Exploration means asking questions, listening with an open mind, and acting. The skills behind these activities are always valuable, but especially in times of transition, when a good sense of life direction is critical. These skills, which serve us at all points on the great cycles of life, begin with the ability to look inward.

The Inner Eye

Successful explorers begin by surveying their interior landscapes. They build self-knowledge before they begin their adventure, and they add to it continually as the trip unfolds. They improve the acuity of their inner eye.

The best way to begin is by looking backward, at life experi-

ence in work and play and love. Sometimes clear insight comes
only years later, but we can always pause and look. Each view,
however clouded, has value.

The purpose of studying the past is to answer questions like:

- What did I do best?
- What did I like best?
- What did I do less well?
- What did I like less well?
- What patterns do I see in my life?
- Where am I now in terms of these patterns?
- What does my past teach me about my talent, knowledge,
  and passion?
- What do my past accomplishments tell me about what I am
  likely to do best in the future?
- How do I feel about what I have done?
- Can I accept the value in my experience?

In answering these questions, a CEO I know discovered that
what he likes best is coaching. His happiest moments are when
he is showing salespeople how to prospect and present and close.
A charismatic leader, he loves to motivate the people who make
his electronic controls, and he feels proudest of the accomplishments achieved through teamwork.

This man is spending more time as coach these days because
he has also spent time pondering questions like these:

- What does each new experience teach me about what I do
  well? About what I like?
- What is there to learn here about the patterns of my life?
- What does this tell me about my talent, knowledge, and passion?
- How do I feel about what is happening here and what does
  this tell me about myself?
- What delights me in this? What surprises me? What fright-
  ens me? What makes me feel this way?
- Behind all the feelings and impressions, who am I? What is
  my reality? Where am I on the cycle and where am I going?

Finally, the inner eye looks at the future. Fantasies, intuitions, inklings, and visions sometimes come unbidden to offer an unstructured view of what lies ahead. This capacity to look into the future can be structured as guided imagery or wish lists or written exercises that free the imagination. It can also come as a dream in the night.

One of my most powerful dreams contained a crucial clue to my first career change. Springing from whatever unconscious place dreams originate, this one focused all the frustration from a troubled time in my life and offered a solution. In the dream I am in Los Angeles to see Jerry West of the Los Angeles Lakers. I go to the 10th floor of a modern office building and meet with West but when I want to leave, the elevator does not come. I wait, with growing anxiety, for 20 minutes. Totally frustrated, I see an old Oriental-looking man and beyond him a door to the stairwell. I know, somehow, to walk through that door and up to the 11th floor, where I immediately get an elevator down.

After the dream I felt relieved, unburdened, and free. Stumbling from bed I realized that there was more than one way to get where I wanted to go, in that Los Angeles office building and in my work. I saw that instead of chasing yet another job in management I could try some other route to fulfillment. Two weeks later I was earnestly seeking a full-time college teaching position. That dream set me free.

Whether insights come in dreams or in other settings, there are rich rewards for studying the future, for looking ahead to get ahead. Consider questions like:

- What do I really want in my future?
- Without my beliefs about my personal limitations, what would my life be like?
- If I could have anything I wanted, what would it be?
- After I got everything I wanted, then what would I want?
- Among the many possibilities for the future, which would be most likely to make me happy?
- What do my dreams for the future tell me about what I should be doing now?
- What do my actions of yesterday and today say about what I really want in the future?

- What draws me forward? What is increasing in relevance for me?
- What draws me less than it used to? What is declining in relevance for me?

Success Strategy: When you hit a bump on the road of life, pull off to the side and ask these questions, to make sure everything is rolling right. Even if you don't hit a bump, do this at least once a year as preventative maintenance.

"The least introspective man I ever knew" is how one executive described Robert Maxwell, the English press baron who drowned in November, 1991, as his empire began to unravel. "He had absolutely no interest in reflection. He never paused. He never listened to others. He was always in motion." For which he paid a heavy price.

You and I are in motion, too. But if we are guided by our inner eye, by our intuition and instincts, we are less likely to encounter the kind of tragedy that brought down Robert Maxwell. If we substitute corrective action for denial, we are more likely to find the right course for fulfilling our purpose in life.

Pioneering

Someone who ventures into unknown or unclaimed territory is called a pioneer. Like the man in Chapter Four who sees himself as a "pioneer of information technology," these people become skillful explorers. Consider these examples from the life of my friend the pioneer:

- At age 11, after researching the best equipment and negotiating the best price, he bought his first printing press.
- After earning an engineering degree, he found a job in printing in order to learn the practical side of the business.
- At age 26 he became an investor for the first time, using his passion for printing to get a taste of ownership.

- In his thirties he started a database publishing company, using leading-edge printing technology.
- In his early forties divorce forced him to become another kind of explorer, eventually leading him to a mate who matched his intellectual intensity and his passion for life.
- At the same time, he was exploring the future of information technology; his research led him to start a company offering legal and regulatory information better and faster than ever before.
- Using both his contacts and his investigatory skills, he took time to find the right American college for the son of a Polish business associate.
- Now approaching his targeted retirement date at age 50, this pioneer is considering the many aspects of making a skillful transition from work to "no more neckties." Always exploring, he is about to start on a new cycle.

Whether you are at the start of your life or contemplating retirement, you will find more success if you are constantly exploring. Whether you are building a new relationship or helping someone find the right college, the skills of exploration will serve you well. Keep looking for the right questions. Keep asking them.

Look for answers in books, newspapers, magazines, trade journals, on radio and TV, in audio tapes. Reach out to people in writing and in person. Use the postal service, electronic mail, modem, fax—whatever tools you can find to ask the questions and look for answers.

As someone said to me recently, the two great virtues in life are love and curiosity. Practice love by being curious—about your life, the lives of others, and the world around you.

Open Minds

Like parachutes, minds don't work unless they're open. As Abraham Lincoln said, "I don't think much of a man who is not wiser today than he was yesterday."

The open mind is one of the most important resources for committed explorers. Green lights are more important to them than red lights, and they make a point of thinking green. They follow the traffic signals of life, responding to serendipitous signals. They seek feedback, both positive and negative, because such input is vital to staying on the path. They look for value in whatever they hear and see, before allowing their mind to close and go on to the next impression.

They may agree with Sir Winston Churchill, who was ready to learn but resistant to teaching. They stay receptive to learning, though, in spite of their fears and biases and old beliefs. They see old problems in new ways. They learn as though they were going to live forever.

There are many kinds of information for explorers in the world of work. There are many areas for learning, most of which fall into these categories:

Kinds of Exploration		Tools for exploration
Inner	{ Past	Success scan, work, autobiography
	Present	Yearnings, likes and dislikes
	Future	Letter in future, obituary exercise
Outer	{ Preliminary	Talking to friends, assessing options
	Focused	Refining plans, conducting exploratory interviews
	Final	Making deals, conducting commitment interviews

Exploration is a major theme of this book and will appear here in many forms. Though few of us ever become world-class at this art, all of us can profit by getting better at it.

People who fully express themselves in their work, people who live on purpose, are continually exploring. Sometimes this is because they sense a need for change; at other times, it is because they are preparing for that moment. When change is at hand, such explorers know how to look until they get what they have learned they need. They know how to convert pain into progress. They know how to get the information and impressions required to take them to the next step, commitment to action.

"We have two choices," Joseph Campbell said, "to live the myth or let the myth live us." Explorers—and you are an explorer if you have read this far—make the right choice.

CHAPTER

8

Commitment

Committing yourself is a way of finding
out who you are.

—Robert Terwilliger

I am not interested in people's claims—
only in what they do. The act came first
and then the word.

—Alfred Stieglitz

Whatever you can do
or dream you can, begin it.
Boldness has genius,
power, and magic in it.

—Goethe

The first 14 years of my professional life were spent scrambling
up the management ladder. The last four years of that period
were spent questioning the climb, as the scrambling got harder
and I slipped a few rungs. Looking up, I sometimes wondered if
my ladder was leaning against the right wall. As part of the questioning I took a job teaching marketing management to MBA
candidates one night a week, and soon found that those three
hours were giving me more joy each week than the 50 hours I
was spending as vice-president of a small company.

But I was not ready to change. After all, my growing up and
my education and my experience all pointed to a career in management. How could I give up all of that?

Then one night, as our family drove through Wyoming toward Yellowstone Park in our VW van, my wife and I talked about what our life would be like if I became a college professor. And she said, "What have you got to lose? Why not try it?"

And I answered, "Why not?"

And so the decision was made. Like a light switch going from off to on, it happened over a few yards of barren highway and cast my whole world in a different perspective. In one magical moment, as our family sped through the darkness, my life and the lives of those around me changed forever.

The search that began with discontent—in my case, with a management career going nowhere—led to exploration and then commitment to change. The decision that had been building for months finally built to the point of commitment. The time came. The choice was made.

No two people arrive at decisions in exactly the same way. For each of us the process is different and for most of us the way we decide changes over the course of our lives. How we decide which milk to buy is different from how we decide on buying a car or buying a company. But the ways you and I make career choices have a lot in common. Based on asking questions of leaders in business and other professions, and my counseling of career changers, both individually and in workshops, I have identified four main ways we arrive at work decisions.

The Plodder

In arriving at decisions, the plodder takes it one easy step at a time. Decision making is a sequential process for plodders; when the process is working, they gather information for one small decision, make it, and then move on to the next small decision. The plodder might work through a series of issues one after the other: Where do I want to live? What kind of work do I want? What kind of company am I interested in? Which job there is right for me? Shall I take this offer?

The skillful plodder develops two areas of self-knowledge: (1) how big a decision to make at any one time and (2) how long to allow for the mini-decisions that lead to big decisions. When the plodder pays attention to these two issues, and makes small enough decisions over a big enough span of time, the results are usually good.

When I was making the decision to become a college professor, my basic style was slow and prodding. That was how I dealt with my fear of making the wrong choice and my reluctance to give up the job I had, despite how unappealing it had become. For me, and for many, the challenge is to keep moving, to overcome procrastination and paralysis.

Skillful plodders learn what decision-making pace is right for them. They learn when to move and when to wait until tomorrow. Though they may miss an occasional fleeting opportunity, skillful plodders learn to recognize attractive openings and act on them. They learn when to take the plunge.

Success Strategy: Make a Commitment to Start. Whatever your decision-making style, begin with small steps. This will bring in new information and allow you to self-correct.

The Plunger

Unlike the plodder, this decision-making type is impulsive and willing to move instantly on the right opportunity. The plunger is confident, impatient, and intuitive. The plunger is a gambler, comfortable in the knowledge that some bets will be losers. Successful plungers, though, hit lots of winners and become better at assessing risk as they accumulate experience.

Sometimes fatalistic, plungers may think, "Whatever will be, will be." Usually they think that their impulsive actions will work out. Their confidence frees them to act. Plungers know instinctively that "boldness has genius, power, and magic in it." The boldness of General H. Norman Schwarzkopf produced magic in the Persian Gulf in 1991.

One reason plungers often make sound long-term decisions is that they have an instinct for focusing on the important questions and letting the small issues resolve themselves. They often have a strong sense of purpose. A plunger who decides to take a new job in a day knows that the size of the office and the length of the commute are much less important than the opportunity offered.

Plungers sometimes operate with little regard for others. My friend Ted once accepted a construction job in Alaska without telling his wife, which illustrates a key point: If there are family members affected by an impulsive decision, plungers soon find that it is important to include them in the decision-making process. While the basic plunging style has many strengths, those who use it successfully over the long term soon come to integrate elements of other styles.

Most of us are plungers in deciding about socks, but not about changing careers. Learn the difference and you will be comfortable in both your footware and your job.

The Strategizer

One decision-making style that is worth integrating into just about any other approach involves strategic thinking. The practitioner of this style asks: What is my purpose and what are the major objectives I must achieve as I move toward it? For each step there are strategies—plans for getting the desired result.

The strategizer knows that to become vice-president of a leading company by age 35 one must have a plan. It must be the right company and the right division and the right boss, all at the right time and place.

One weakness skillful strategizers learn to overcome is rigid adherence to a plan. Conditions change, people change, times change and sometimes that calls for a whole new response. That may be time to create a new plan, one with built-in flexibility. Dennis, a strategizer extraordinaire, generated a job offer from a competitor, developed a scenario for buying part of the company he works for, and figured out how to start his own business—all at the same time.

Strategizers need to be wary of relying too heavily on rational processes. Not all knowledge is derived through logic, and most people who continue to use a strategizing style come to rely on their emotions and intuition as well as their reasoning ability.

The best strategizers, in fact, rely heavily on the synthesis of divergent positions and points of view in making decisions about work and life.

The Synthesizer

The final decision-making type is one who integrates elements from each of the other four. In making decisions the synthesizer is likely to seek input from a plodder, to make sure nothing has been missed, and perhaps even a procrastinator. Synthesizers listen to plungers (but don't usually leap precipitously) and strategizers (because they want to be sure they have applied sufficient logic). Then they make their own decision.

The synthesizer is vulnerable to becoming swept away by the preponderance of opinion, which is not always right. Skillful synthesizers make sure they take time to check their own instincts as well as those of others they respect.

Plodder, plunger, strategizer, synthesizer. Each style has its advantages depending on the decision faced and the inclinations of the decision maker. There is no one best style, though successful people often blend styles, like this:

PLODDER · PLUNGER

STRATEGIZER · SYNTHESIZER

When I was making the decision in 1976 to go into academia, I synthesized diverse input and approaches into my basic plodding style. Because I was attending workshops and reading books like *What Color Is Your Parachute?* I also did a lot of strategizing. When I make work decisions now, I take time to think back over my experiences to make sure I am using the process that works best for me. How about you?

Exploration: How Do I Commit? Think back to the last important decision you made. List as many steps as you can think of that led to that decision. When did you actually commit? What does this tell you about your decision-making style? How can you strengthen your style?

Magic happens when we step over the line from "Wouldn't this be nice?" to "Yes, I'll do it"—and no one expressed it better than William Murray, whose commitment in 1950 took him to the top of several Himalayan peaks. We committed ourselves, he wrote, when we "had put down our passage money—booked a sailing for Bombay." This may sound too simple, Murray continued, but it is great in consequence because:

> Until one is committed there is hesitancy, the chance to draw back, always ineffectiveness. Concerning all acts of initiative (and creation), there is one elementary truth, the ignorance of which kills countless ideas and splendid plans: that the moment one definitely commits oneself, then Providence moves too. All sorts of things occur to help one that would never otherwise have occurred. A whole stream of events issues from the decision, raising in one's favor all manner of unforseen incidents and meetings and material assistance, which no man could have dreamt would have come his way.

Nothing happens until we commit. All the great plans in the world are meaningless unless there is commitment and action. There are many ways to arrive at this moment, whether we are plodders, plungers, synthesizers, or strategizers, whether we make our decision with our family or in quiet contemplation. Whatever our style and however we come to the decision point, what really matters is that we step to the mark and take the leap.

9

Low Points, Change Points

Sighs, lamentations and loud wailing
resounded through the starless air, so that
at first it made me weep; strange tongues,
horrible language, words of pain, tones of
anger, voices loud and hoarse, and with
these the sound of hands, made a tumult
which is whirling through that air forever
dark, as sand eddies in a whirlwind.

—Dante, *Inferno*

To live is to change; to be perfect is to
have changed often.

—Cardinal Newman

"Fear is a universal experience," says philosopher Jacob Needleman. "We all feel it." How can we handle fear? "Identify it, acknowledge it for what it is. Fear named is fear defused. Then get more data, because 95 percent of the problems we face can be solved with the right information."

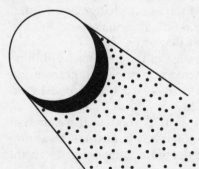

In the great cycle, nothing is more fearsome than the bottom, the immersion into unknown waters of unfathomable depths. We go down without knowing how far. Behind seems long ago and ahead is mist and "starless air." It is the dark side of the moon, total black-ness.

More than any other point on the cycle, the bottom is a place of change. Fueled by fear, it is a time of releasing old beliefs and perceptions. It is a time of giving up old attitudes without having proven replacements. It is a time with enormous potential for learning, though the lessons rarely come easy.

How do you know you're at the bottom? Those who have been there report that:

- Feelings are heightened, crashing in like breakers.
- Everything looks different, mainly worse.
- You're bewildered, disoriented, in shock.
- You're discouraged, demotivated.
- You're depressed, questioning the value of living.
- Your beliefs no longer seem meaningful.
- Friends treat you differently, keeping their distance.
- It seems like the darkness will never end.
- Life feels like hell.
- Like Dante, you hear words of pain.
- Like Job, you no longer feel human.

Hades

Two days after Christmas in 1985 I visited Hades, the bottom of the cycle, the land of the dead. I went where Inanna had been, where Odysseus had been. I was at the change point—shall I cling to my tenured professorship or leave the college? Am I re-ally going to die or do I just feel that way?

That Friday night I sat on the edge of the bed, my head in my hands, my heart in a hole, immersed in depression, despair, and blackness. Hades, the underworld of horrors described by the ancients, where I feared for my life.

In the darkness I found clarity: "It is right to leave the col-lege." Clear and sure, without ambiguity, I knew that it was time to move on. Pain produced the decision. Pain pointed out the path.

"Come with us, John," said my wife, reaching out a hand for

me, and up I came, comforted by new insight and relieved to be back in the land of the living. My wife and daughter and I went to a San Francisco Ballet performance of "The Nutcracker" that night, and the action has never been so vivid. The music was more beautiful, the costumes more colorful, the opera house more spectacular than ever before. I was reborn.

The Dark Night

At the bottom of the cycle, in the land of change, after commitment and before renewal comes the dark night of the soul.

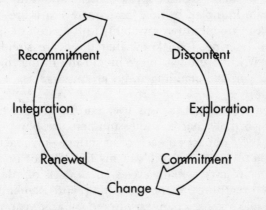

This is the territory of the supreme ordeal—traversed by Inanna, Odysseus, and Job and familiar to many of us. There are those who never go to the bottom, seeing it only through the eyes of others. There are those who live on the edge, spending so many years in discontent they lose the motivation to move. Some go into this territory at the bottom of the cycle with a work crisis and some with a love crisis.

For some it's a combination of love and work. Like Christine who confessed, "When my marriage was breaking up I found myself sharing more and more with my boss. I could tell him things I never told anyone before and I looked forward to going to work each day just so we could spend time together."

It was not destined to last. "When business started to dry up he got more and more irritable," she sighs. "Then we went into Chapter 11 and I realized I'd lost both the job and the relationship. I was *in extremis.*"

She stayed there for months, living on alimony and a small inheritance, not looking for work, not dating. Only when Christine decided to get the college degree she had abandoned in her twenties did she emerge from the darkness. She came back to a place when she had been happy—the classroom—and once again found purpose in her life.

More than any other point on the journey, the bottom is different for each of us. More than any other point, it is a solitary experience, an inner, private experience difficult to explain and impossible to share. When I speak or write about my visits to the bottom, I am humbled by how inadequate words are—the experience is vastly deeper than my ability with written or spoken language can describe. I do know that there are some things to remember if you are down there or moving in that direction or if, like me, you are planning to go around again.

• **Cycles are natural,** in our lives and in the universe. Some winters are brutally harsh, some summers are bone dry. Cycles differ and their impact on each of us differs—my reaction to the cycles of nature and the cycles in my life will not be yours. But the presence of cycles, many cycles, in all parts of our lives, is as natural as breathing in and breathing out. Remember "Rule No. 1" of making big changes, offered by a 33-year-old woman who has been there: "Be completely emotional—cry as much as you want, laugh as much as you can. You are throwing yourself into the world of the unknown. If you bottle everything up, you will just go nuts."

• **Cycles are for learning,** about ourselves, about our purpose, about life. Learning can only happen when we "unfreeze," when our preconceptions are cracked and prejudices softened. At the bottom of the cycle we learn, we change, we are transformed. Once we start out again, once we know the relief of escape and the joy of renewal, we are less receptive to new ways of thinking and being. We "refreeze" until the next cycle.

• **We do come out.** However we go into the bottom of the cycle—whether we dive, jump, or are pushed—we eventually emerge. Even at the end of the great cycle called life, philosophers tell us, there is reincarnation or afterlife or heaven. In the cycles of work and love, too, we are reborn and one of the benefits of this rebirth is that we become part of the community of the twice-born. We are initiates. We have been there, we recognize others who have been there, and we know the joy of coming out.

Coming Out

When we are at the bottom there are five steps to starting out again, usually occurring in this sequence:

1. **Reach out.** People will often extend a hand, and unless we reach out and take it we risk drowning. No matter how low we feel, we must act—respond to an offer of help, call a friend, schedule a meeting with an adviser. The career counselor I once sought out in a time of despair told me I was on the right course and gave me the courage to go on. A sincere request for help is rarely rejected.
2. **Assess.** An honest appraisal of where we are is a big step toward moving to somewhere better. This is the time for acknowledging ourselves, a time for candor about how we feel and how we see our prospects, a time for open eyes and accessible hearts. As I contemplated leaving my college job I talked to teachers and trustees as well as with authors and consultants who were doing what I hoped to do.
3. **Create options.** Even the bleakest picture presents choices. Look for them. Clarify them. Ask friends for ideas. Figure out how practical and affordable they are. Consider all possibilities and then write about the three or four most appealing. Transition consultant William Bridges calls this a time of high creativity, a life stage when we see things to which we are blind at other times. Look for these possibilities. Record your good ideas. And consider some of the best advice I ever got: The day you start a new career, begin preparing for the next one.
4. **Act.** The best antidote for depression is action, however small, however subtle, however inconsequential. Take a first

step. Indulge your curiosity. Make a plan. Call a friend. Write someone to develop an option. The journey of a thousand miles needs to begin somewhere.

5. **Care for yourself.** Eat right. Exercise. Smell the roses. Laugh and cry. Play with friends. Get some mental health time with a compassionate listener. Care for your body and soul during this demanding transition. I did all of this and still felt the stress. But I also did something I exhort you to do: take a break between careers. Mine was a nine-month trip to Europe. Even if yours can only be a few weeks or a few days, do it. You will have LOTS of time to work.

EXPLORATION: What Is the Bottom Like for Me? Write a description, with as many facts and dates and specific feelings as you can remember, of the last time you were there. Now draw a picture of it, focusing on how you felt and what you saw, rather than artistic quality. You've read what I learned from this exploration; now it's your turn.

After plunging, we bottom out. We reach the low point and begin our return from the cold, dark depths. Our spirit may be drenched and our perspective gloomy. We may not see it but before us lies the potential for a journey into the sunlight. The sage is right: the night is darkest just before the dawn.

Coming out of the darkness, out of the change point at the bottom of the cycle, we bring a gift, "an elixer, a boon that restores the world," in the words of Joseph Campbell. Hope, enthusiasm, passion are some of the boons people bring from the depths; also insight, confidence, perspective, and wisdom.

What kind of boon might one discover? Consider three boon bearers who went to the bottom of the cycle early in life. All are explorers, survivors, exemplars. Each brings a special gift.

Joshua Roth earned a five-year degree in architecture and worked for seven years in small companies designing homes. On his thirty-second birthday he was laid off. He rode his bike to the nearby American Institute of Architects office to inquire about other jobs. No luck. On the return ride he stopped at a bike shop to see if someone who had loved biking most of his life could get a job. "When can you start?" he was asked. "Tomorrow!" he replied, deciding on a career change that led to happiness, fulfillment, and full employment. His fantasy is to build his own bikes, using what he learned in architecture to create wonderful aesthetics—creating a boon for bike lovers and others, too.

Margot Fraser was concerned mainly with survival in 1970 when she divorced. She was thinking of returning to the profession her father had recommended years earlier, dressmaking. But people kept asking about the Birkenstock sandals she had introduced in this country four years earlier and she made her fateful call to Karl Birkenstock. Yes, he would be willing to do business with a woman. Yes, he would visit European art museums with Fraser to see how sandals had evolved over the centuries. And, yes, he was delighted when Fraser the former dressmaker had design suggestions that made Birkenstocks world class.

George Conlan went bankrupt at age 27. Returning with an honorable discharge from Army service in Korea, he found that the tire company he and a partner started three years before was beyond saving. He emerged from that low point with a new wife and a new job, a job that eventually led him to the presidency of the leading orange juice distributor in northern California. Besides bringing the boon of healthy dining, the company Conlan headed produced successful executives for his and several other companies—a boon that keeps on giving.

Whatever form our boon takes, the gift is one we have had all along but only now bring fully into the light. Our pain becomes a blessing, the source of transformation. Our time in the darkness generates brightness to illuminate our lives and the lives of others.

CHAPTER

10

Renewal: The High That Binds

This is the noble truth of the arising
of sorrow. It arises from craving,
which leads to rebirth, which brings
delight and passion.

—The Pali Canon

To yield is to be preserved whole.
To be bent is to become straight.
To be empty is to be full.
To be worn out is to be renewed.

—Lao-tzu

Long ago and far away, in a country beyond the sea beyond the sea, lived a wise and well-loved woman who possessed a pearl of inestimable value. In the course of her travels this woman had to traverse a barren desert on whose edge she camped while obtaining provisions. On the night before her departure a stranger appeared and the wise and well-loved woman asked if he would like to be her companion on the six-day journey.

"Of course," he replied for (though few knew it) he was a thief who lusted after the pearl of inestimable value.

At the end of the first day when the woman went out into the desert for her evening meditation, the thief searched everywhere for the pearl—in the baggage, in the food containers, in the map case, all without success.

Again at the end of the second day, when the woman went

alone into the desert, the thief searched and searched, in the lining of the saddles, in the camel's ear, everywhere. And still no pearl, that night or the three that followed.

When the two reached the far side of the desert, the wise and well-loved woman said to the man, "You have been a good companion and I would like you to have this gold piece as an expression of my appreciation."

"Alas," said he, "I cannot take your gold for in fact I am a thief who each night searched your belongings for the pearl of inestimable value."

"Please take the coin," she said, smiling. "You earned it. Because each night when I went out from camp I left the pearl, for safekeeping, beneath your pillow."

After a trip through the desert is a good time to check under the pillow. What we usually find is that the treasure we sought from others—friends, teachers, bosses, mentors—was ours all along. We discover that the pearl of our own individuality, our boon for the world, is within us. The treasure we seek is the treasure we already possess. The attributes we long for, those we truly need, are already ours. As with any discovery, this brings joy and excitement, a feeling of rebirth, of delight, and passion.

Renewal

How do you know you're in a renewal phase? You are probably in renewal if you can look back and say, "Wow, I've just been through something big." Especially if that something threatened to change your life, and particularly if it did. Some other ways you know are:

- The world looks bright and fresh.
- You feel fortunate, relieved, grateful.
- You feel uplifted, euphoric, with a sense of well-being.
- You are optimistic and positive.
- You are confident, capable, full of energy.
- You feel everything you *didn't* feel at the bottom of the cycle.

- Friends respond to you with new affection, warmth, and respect.
- Like Job, your vision grows. "I have heard of thee by the hearing of the ear," Job says in the Bible, "but now mine eye seeth thee."

What's renewal? It's the exuberance you feel coming back from a great trip or weekend retreat or wonderful night at the theater. It's when you are high and excited and your enthusiasm spills over onto those around you. "You should do what I just did," you tell them, undeterred by skeptics.

Your experience rubs off on others, even if you are by nature one of the world's quiet people. Those around you sense what you have been through and see how you have come out of it. It helps if you tell them, but it isn't necessary. They know.

Renewal is an interpersonal phenomenon as well as an interior experience. As Lucretius said more than 2,000 years ago, "The sum of things is ever being renewed, and mortals live dependent upon one another." We depend on our fellow humans to complete the cycle of death and rebirth, again and again, and we share the joys of renewal in the lives of those around us. Our common experiences in that cycle bind us one to the other.

Repotting

Some of the most telling imagery for renewal comes from nature and the best of all, I think, comes from the world of roses, as businessman Ernie Arbuckle showed us, using his own life as the illustration. Arbuckle's first career began at what is now Chevron Corporation and continued after World War II at W. R. Grace, where he rose to the position of executive vice-president. For career number two he moved to academia, as dean of the Stanford Business School. At age 56 he moved again, accepting the chairmanship of Wells Fargo Bank, and, 10 years later, the chairmanship of Saga Corporation—where he was serving when he died in a 1986 automobile accident.

Arbuckle loved his garden, and especially his roses, so it was natural for him to link career growth to the tending of flowers. In a 1980 interview he told me:

> They talk about me repotting myself every few years and that analogy is apt. I enjoy changing challenges, changing jobs, changing my environment and it seems to me it's just like a flowering plant in a new location.
>
> I garden when I have the time and I notice that I give the new plants special attention. They get fresh soil and injections of fertilizer. They start to look healthy and flourish. It works for those plants just as it has worked for me.

The special attention we get offers special opportunities during the renewal phase. With people, as with roses, there are new ways to flourish.

Extra energy lets us do things we are less able or less likely to do at other points on the cycle. New brooms sweep with more vigor. When the cleaning is done purposefully, the results can be extraordinary. An extra class load was a joy for me when I first started teaching, as was the chance to start a business department, counsel career changers, and chaperone school dances.

New innocence lets us do things we didn't know were impossible. Before our mind fills with limitations we attempt tasks the culture will later discourage. As an academic, I didn't know the 1,000 reasons an overseas study program couldn't happen, so I started one at Oxford University. Later, when our eyes are opened to organizational realities, we are less likely to take such risks.

Extra time presents special opportunities in new jobs. There are things we can do and lessons we can learn before we are fully into our new responsibilities, by using our extra energy and the time-saving strategies we bring with us. Later we will be more likely to want any extra time for ourselves.

New insights based on earlier experience enable us to contribute in unique ways. The business background I brought to academia helped me in recruiting prospective students, for instance, and in managing people. The same thing can happen for you.

Success Strategy: Honor Exuberance. Those in the renewal phase are often exuberant, full of energy and new ideas. Honor this in yourself and others. As William Blake said, "Exuberance is beauty."

Rebirth

Coming up from the dark days of December 1985, I was reborn. There were shaky moments and unsure steps as I left the academic womb. But there was awe and wonder, too. Then there was the transcendent moment when the seniors asked me to give the address the following spring at their commencement—a celebration of the beginning of new lives for them and for me.

My new professional life began as I signed the lease on my office. Another high. Then the joy of my first consulting assignment, the excitement of leading the annual retreat for a major law firm at Pebble Beach, and the rush when my second book, *The Right Work,* was published in the fall of 1987. It was a time of high energy, of renewal and rebirth, the joyful, sparkling side of the cycle.

EXPLORATION: How Do I Celebrate Renewal? Create a congratulatory certificate for yourself, celebrating the last time you went through renewal. Add color and a seal and an elaborate border. Show your certificate to a friend.

In describing the heroic journey, Joseph Campbell said that the return from the depths could be either volitional or in flight from powerful forces. It could be on the traveler's initiative or it could be escape. Either way, it was a dangerous time, sometimes made easier by helpers, but always full of risks.

Whatever the return is like, and it is different in every heroic journey, it is an integral part of a vital process. As Campbell says:

> Only birth can conquer death. . . . Within the soul, within the body social, there must be—if we are to experience long survival—a continuous "recurrence of birth" to nullify the unremitting recurrences of death.

11

Integration: Heading Home

You can't go home again.

—Thomas Wolfe

The truth of the matter is that you *always* know the right thing to do. The hard part is doing it.

—General H. Norman Schwarzkopf

Not this time and yet not that time but one time, in the Italian town of Pisa, a beautiful young maiden climbed the famous Leaning Tower and in her rapture over the view leaned too far out and tumbled over the rail. That night her mourning fiancé dreamed that he encountered his beloved in heaven.

"Tell me about your fall," he said in the dream.

"The impact was terrible," she sighed, "but the trip—oh, the trip was terrific."

Since everyone on the planet arrives at the same ultimate destination—and who can say how terrible it will be?—the action question for each of us is: What am I doing to make the trip terrific?

Terrific Trips

Integration is getting it all together. It is taking the lessons learned through the cycle, including those from renewal, and making them ours. It is accepting our practical limitations, at work and in life, and minimizing them or even turning them into strengths. It is our return to reality as we head toward home again.

We know we are in this life phase when the glow of renewal starts to fade and the euphoria of emerging from the darkness becomes less immediate. We move from the altered state of renewal to the familiar feel of places we started from. We return, but not as the same person. Our view of the world is different and our store of wisdom is enlarged. We are changed by the experiences of the adventure.

The journey itself provides all we need for these changes. If we look inside as we travel along the path, if we look at the road signs and clues on the trail, we will see all we require to correct our course and make the rest of the trip terrific. We will have what we need to live our life on purpose.

We do not need the canoe we used to cross rivers earlier in the journey or the lifeline we used to climb mountains. Carrying extra equipment weighs us down and detracts from the rest of the trip. But the *experience* of the rivers and mountains of life adds satisfaction and success in the miles ahead.

Five questions help with integration, in this sequence:

1. **What do I want more of, this time around?** Even though my life has changed, my most basic longings have not. What activities do I want to keep in my life or find more of? What emotional rewards can I build into my life? Now that I know more about myself, what psychic satisfactions should I seek?

2. **What do I want less of, this time around?** Based on the pain of discontent, on my struggles over the downward slope of the cycle, what activities do I now want less of in my work life? I know people who have given up being physicians, lawyers, accountants, and supervisors in order to create more fulfilling lives. How about you?

3. **What am I hiding from myself that could keep this time around from being wonderful?** What delusions, rationalizations, and obsessions were not left behind when I emerged from the dark? If I am totally honest with myself, where am I constrained? Perhaps you, like me, are confused about money and feel you ought to earn as much as your friends—which I just realized is for me is a big, burdensome ego trip.

4. **What do I still want to change?** This doesn't mean becoming a new person but it does mean liking yourself better as the trip continues. Life becomes more pleasant for us and for those around us if we continue to grow and evolve. As I let go of my need to impress others with my earnings, I notice that life gets better.

5. **Where is my joy?** Am I having as much fun as I'd like? Am I laughing enough? Am I proud of what I am accomplishing? Am I aligned with my purpose in life? These questions can be asked anytime, but they are particularly poignant as we settle back into life routines after times of intense change.

Success Strategy: Celebrate Success. Mark achievements in your own life and in the lives of those you love with cards, parties, rituals, and ceremonies. Take the time to note the good points in life. Make them special.

Successful travelers learn along the way. They adjust, find new allies, use resources in different ways. They also learn to accept the fact that they are more human than otherwise.

Foibles and Foolishness

The Procter & Gamble Company runs by numbers—case sales, share points, profit dollars; big numbers, small numbers, pages and pages of numbers. If you work at P & G, as I did early in my business career, you generate lots of numbers, especially as a beginner. There are numbers to manage your part of the business, numbers for the sales department, and numbers that eventually, if they are right, add up to your next promotion.

The trouble is, I'm better at people than I am at numbers. Was then and am now. After a couple of months behind the standard issue Monroe calculator in the bull pen on the 9th floor of the Procter & Gamble building in Cincinnati, the mistakes I was making became a problem.

"That's ten cents off the king size, not the giant size, John, in the Houston district next March."

"The media plan for next year is 20 spots for 10 weeks in the top five markets, not 10 spots for 20 weeks."

"Can't you get this right?"

Yes, of course, I could get it right, by redoing my calculations, by cross-checking, by taking more time—usually between six and nine in the evening. Did fewer mistakes make me a better management prospect at P & G? Not really, I realized, and the extra hours at the Monroe calculator were not adding joy to my family life, either. That's when I realized it was time for a change and began the process that led me to work for smaller companies and eventually to a new career as a college professor.

I still have trouble getting the right number of zeros when I multiply big numbers, and I still get my facts turned around once in a while. But these foibles are less troublesome now, to me and to those with whom I work, than they were at a giant company run by numbers. Each change since Procter & Gamble took me away from big numbers and toward more people involvement, until today I have the right balance.

Whatever our foibles and whatever our foolishness, we need to accept ourselves as we are. We need to appreciate our positives along with our negatives, to honor the silver lining in the clouds over our lives. We need to put our talent to work in settings where our limitations are less important and where our strengths count. We know the right thing to do, says General Schwarzkopf; the hard part is doing it. When we accept ourselves, the doing becomes easier.

The company presidents with whom I work are familiar with the poem *Ulysses*, by Alfred Tennyson, whose words make this point beautifully:

> That which we are, we are
> One equal measure of heroic hearts
> Made weak by time and fate,
> Yet strong in will
> To strive, to seek, to find,
> And not to yield.

Look Homeward

When Thomas Wolfe wrote *Look Homeward, Angel*, he described alienation and despair. He showed that the home we return to is not the same home we leave. The literal, physical place is never the same . . . except symbolically, except as a representation of mother love and father love and unconditional acceptance. If our time away has been fruitful, the symbolic home to which we return is safer and more welcome than ever before.

EXPLORATION: What Are My Strengths? What character traits and skills got me here? What inner resources and valor served me through the bottom of the cycle? Make a list on the left-hand side of a sheet of paper and on the right note how you are using these strengths in your life today.

We cannot go home again, not to the same home we left, but we can return to a new and better place, a place we appreciate in new ways because, having been around the cycle this time, we know that we will go around again. We can continue to learn and grow. We can find joy in change. Like the beautiful young maiden from Pisa we can declare at the end, "The trip was terrific."

CHAPTER

12

Love Made Visible

Going on means going far.
Going far means returning.

—*Tao Te Ching*

There is a tide in the affairs of man which,
taken on the flood leads to fortune;
omitted, all the voyage of their life is
bound in shallows and in miseries; and we
must take the current when it serves or
lose our ventures.

—Shakespeare

Work is love made visible.

—Kahlil Gibran

" 'I realize you're never going to be happy unless you're doing things you think are worthwhile,' my wife said to me the other day." This from a 70-year-old leader who touched many lives in each of his careers. "I was touched ... because she's right."

Repotting took Ernie Arbuckle from Chevron to Stanford to Wells Fargo Bank. Twelve years after returning to industry he talked about the importance of "doing things you think are worthwhile."

Worthwhile? "I want to keep my attention on the problems of others, not on my own," said Arbuckle, who was chairman of Saga Corporation at the time. He was also serving on the Executive Service Board and "You don't get paid for that," he told me. "Well, you do, but not in money."

For Arbuckle, service was a part of life. He committed to it, he recommitted. He rededicated his energies on each of his several trips through the career cycle, did so because he believed in living fully and because he was determined to continue growing, like the roses in his garden.

Like Ernie Arbuckle, you and I can recommit as we near the home place at the top of the cycle and head toward the discontent that surely lies ahead.

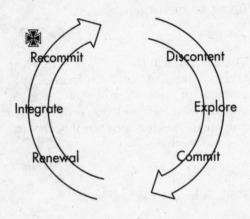

Success Strategy: Empower Your Life with Commitment. Use the power of your dedication, openly expressed, to enlist others in achieving noble purposes. Express commitment in words and pictures and actions. Recommit often.

Choices

A friend of mine always plans one vacation ahead. He and his wife agree on where they're going next year while they're still in the vacation mood in Hawaii or Italy or wherever they happen to be this year. Life planning works this way, too. The moment we're nearing the top is the best time to decide to go off again in pursuit of our purpose. The best time to commit to the next journey is as we head home.

Actually, we have three choices:

1. **We can decide not to go around again.** This is enough, we may conclude. No more. Sometimes this works, but usually events conspire to create something different. We run into discontent again and because we know the power of committing to change, that's what we do. Around again we go, despite ourselves. Or we retire from a longtime job and find ourselves with new challenges, new experiences, new cycles. Deciding not to go around again rarely works.

2. **We can make no decision** and just let whatever happens, happen. This is what most people do and it often works. When we next encounter discontent we are better prepared because we've been that way before. But failing to plan is still planning to fail, which is why successful people choose the third option.

3. **We can recommit.** We can decide consciously, even publicly, that we will go around again. By expressing this intention, if only to ourselves, we add power to our lives and improve our chances of enjoying a better trip next time. We commit ourselves to a plan, we commit ourselves to a purpose, we commit ourselves to a vision of how we would like our future to be. This attracts energy, sometimes in ways we cannot anticipate, and adds meaning to each day.

The rest of this chapter and much of the rest of this book is about commitment and recommitment, about pursuing your purpose and achieving your vision. As you travel through these pages you will see many ways to add value to your life by taking action on what you are learning.

Learning

What puts us in a position to commit and recommit is new insights and information. We learn how to change, how to manage change, how to respond to change, how to live our purpose. Real change is not easy for any of us, but in the world of work it is probably most difficult for those in the fields of medicine and religion.

This is why the life-change strategies pursued by Archbishop John Quinn are so instructive. Quinn, who decided to be a priest when he was eight years old, explains, "I became a priest to give my life to God serving people." He did not seek the position he holds now as the sixth archbishop of San Francisco, in charge of 375,000 parishioners, a major school system, and extensive social service agencies.

"I encourage continuing education," he told me when I met with him in 1986. Taking his own advice, he left San Francisco in late 1987 on a "sabbatical" to "learn how to deal more effectively with problems of stress." Quinn spent five months in retreat at the Institute of Living in Hartford, Connecticut, the nation's largest private psychiatric hospital, dealing with burnout and, in his words, "an increasing and prolonged depression." Perhaps this servant of God had been trying to do too much, perhaps he was at the end of a cycle. When he returned to his job, it was clear that he had learned a lot and that his sabbatical had changed him.

What is the renewed John Quinn like?

"I no longer feel that I have to deal with everything that comes along," he said in a newspaper interview. "I know my own limitations now, which brings a lot of composure in the face of all the overwhelming problems that are always coming at me. I know now that I can't be perfect. Nobody can." Powerful learning for any of us, precious insights from a reflective life.

"You feel tremendous responsibility," says Quinn, who in his sixties is a vital link between the Vatican and American bishops. "These issues coming at you are very important ones. But you come to understand that you're not the Lord, only a servant of the Lord."

What can you and I learn from John Quinn?

The importance of change and the value of candor, for starters; also how to retreat and come back renewed and recommitted. Like Quinn, we can define and deal with our limitations. We can improve our perspective on the challenges before us and heighten our understanding of where we fit in. We can emulate John Quinn, who stayed true to his calling through stress and depression, who in his mission of service never forgot his purpose.

Purpose

Purpose enriches the journey over life's hills and dales, whether it is a five-month retreat in a psychiatric hospital or a 10-year repotting cycle. If we have some idea of what we are about, the trip makes more sense. Knowing who we are and why we are here adds to the experience. Whether our purpose is to serve the Lord, create healthy homes, or to build the best personal computer, we are ennobled by its pursuit. The seven steps to finding your purpose at the beginning of this book and your travels through life's cycles are all about discovering what to pursue.

Even if we don't have the words and images quite right yet, our efforts to define the purpose of our journey add meaning. This can give a third dimension to the trip, turning the cycles into a helix, spiraling upward toward our life vision.

When life is an ascending spiral it becomes love made visible. "And what is it to work with love?" the Prophet is asked in Kahlil Gibran's masterpiece:

It is to weave the cloth with threads drawn from your heart, even as if your beloved were to wear that cloth.

It is to build a house with affection, even as if your beloved were to dwell in that house.

It is to sow seeds with tenderness and reap the harvest with joy, even as if your beloved were to eat the fruit.

It is to change all things you fashion with a breath of your own spirit,

And to know that all the blessed dead are standing about you and watching.

EXPLORATION: What Are My Commitments? To what principles and purposes, actions and results are you committed? Write your commitments on a card and put your name at the top along with the date. Tape it over your desk.

Imagine that there is a club whose members are committed to making their work lives better. There are many members, full of energy and enthusiasm, and there is no discrimination based on age, race, religion, sexual preference, or the number of mistakes made in the past. You have already paid your dues, many times over. Those in the club are prepared to welcome you with open arms. The membership committee approves of you, unconditionally.

Are you ready to join? Are you willing to be committed? Are you ready for change in your life? The club is there. The choice is yours.

PART

III

Making Plans

CHAPTER

13

Find Yourself, Forget Yourself

Ask, and it shall be given to you; Seek,
and ye shall find; Knock and it shall be
opened unto you.

—Matthew 7:7

I like what is in work—the chance to find
yourself. Your own reality—for yourself,
not for others—what no outsider can ever
know.

—Joseph Conrad

Who you are is God's gift to you.
Who you become is your gift to God.

—Esalen workshop leader

"People think I'm crazy," says Arsenio Hall, "but I was put here to do what I'm doing." Some of us know sooner, some of us later, what we were put here to be doing. All of us need to consider the question, eventually, if we want value and meaning in our lives.

How did it work for Arsenio? "I planned it. That's the only way I could beat the odds." Pondering his success as a talk-show host and comic, he is sure that the way his life has evolved is more than coincidence.

For those of us who didn't have a plan, or whose plans have

fizzled, the next best thing is to start on the basic questions: What do I do best? Where should I be doing it? How does my thing fit in the world around me?

Finding work is a process of self-discovery; so is life itself. The more willing we are to discover the truth, the more effective we become, in work and in our personal life.

One way to understand what you are best at doing is to inventory your gifts. Think of these as birthday gifts, just for you, because you are special. One or two may be from unexpected sources; most will be surprises when you open them. All will give you pleasure, some will give you lasting joy. Let today be your birthday and tear the wrappings off the gifts you bring to your work. Open up the boxes and discover what it is that makes it possible for you to do what you do best.

The gifts you will find fall into three main categories: talents, knowledge, and passions.

Talent and Knowledge

Talent is a gift, a unique inheritance we are given at birth for shaping and developing over the course of our lives. Talent is actually many, many gifts shaped from birth by experimentation, education, work, and living. Your job is to identify your gifts, especially those you want to use regularly or strengthen further.

Your talent reflects many skills, big ones and small ones, some 700, in fact, for the average person, according to job-finding authority Richard Bolles. Skills are what you can do, and motivated skills, the kind you care about most, are what you are inspired to do.

In developing your skills, in building on your native talent, you have learned a lot. This is called knowledge, and it is just as important as talent. Knowledge is what you know, such as how to direct someone across town or the batting averages for the New York Yankees.

As you identify your gifts you will notice that talents and areas of knowledge sometimes overlap, like this:

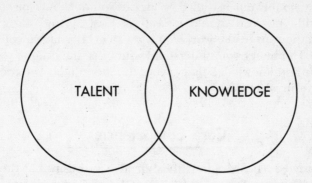

Consider Arsenio Hall. Born in 1959, he undoubtedly inherited some acting talent from his father, a Baptist preacher. His obsession with watching television was not so unusual in the Cleveland neighborhood where he grew up, but the other kids were not entertaining their mothers with commentaries on Dick Cavett and Johnny Carson.

Arsenio developed skills interviewing neighborhood kids with the walkie-talkie his mother gave him. TV expanded his knowledge of people and what makes them laugh. When he started in Los Angeles as a $10 a night stand-up comic, this talent and knowledge helped him succeed. And keep succeeding.

"This feels *goooooood!*" Arsenio likes to say to those in his audience, many of whom formerly watched Cavett and Carson. If asked what makes him a popular talk-show host, Arsenio might start with skills and knowledge like this:

Skills	*Knowledge*
Entertaining	What makes people laugh
• Telling stories	What makes people cry
• Mimicking	Television talk shows
• Acting	Television production
Interviewing	Movie production
• Questioning	American politics
• Listening	Black entertainers
• Supporting	Black sensibilities

How would your list start? What can you do? (You may not list 700 skills, but you should identify at least 50, including those most important in the work you want to do.) What do you know about? The better you understand your gifts, the unique package of skills and knowledge that is you, the more likely you are to be effective in your work.

Core Competencies

"Have you heard about the hot idea in business?" the CEO asked. "Here is the *Harvard Business Review,*" she said. "It's called core competence, what a company does best." The article, by C. K. Prahalad and Gary Hamel, says core competence is "the collective learning of the organization."

What works for business often works for persons, as this "hot idea" illustrates. Individuals have core competencies, just like organizations, based on their cumulative learning. Consider these individual equivalents of the competencies described by Prahalad and Hamel.

Examples of Core Competencies

Organizational Version	Individual Equivalent
"Provide potential access to a wide variety of markets"	Provide capacity to serve a wide variety of needs
"Make a contribution to the customer benefits of the product"	Make a contribution to those for whom you work
"Are difficult for competitors to imitate"	Are what make your contributions unique

What are *your* core competencies? What gives you a special capacity to serve? Given your cumulative learning, what special contributions can you make? How does your unique experience make you different from others who aspire to contribute?

Passion and Purpose

The best gift of all, the one that adds punch to your talent and power to your competence, is the passion you bring to your work. Like a sunrise, passion comes in various hues, ranging from pale and subtle to bright and intense. Passion goes from mild interest, to thoughtful concern, to all-consuming obsession. Sometimes identified by vocational counselors as "interests," it is also less than that and much, much more. Passion moves us to action; passion is our highest motivator.

Passion may be general, like "doing quality work" or "making a positive contribution each day." It may be specific like "teaching learning disabled children" or "creating interactive software" or "making people laugh." Pieces of our passion are easy to identify—most of us can name a number of interests, for instance—but the core of our passion is harder to define, and sometimes takes years to understand.

For me, at least, it has taken a long time. After lots of mistakes and much bumbling I now realize how much I care about excellence and about helping people. Ideas are vitally important to me, too, and I love to connect people with one another and with ideas that lead to action. At the heart of my passion—and this has changed very little over the last decade—is the right work, for myself and for others. This is how I see it now, though I still look through imperfect lenses.

In arriving at these insights I've done pages of writing, spent hours in workshops, and had solid counseling help. I've also helped lots of others and learned volumes in the process. Alone and in workshops and counseling sessions I've spent hours and hours pondering my passion.

How about you? Where is the heart of your passion? What do you care most about? It is never too early to start asking this question. It is never too late to let passion turbocharge your life.

As the last of the three great gift categories, passion overlaps with the other two:

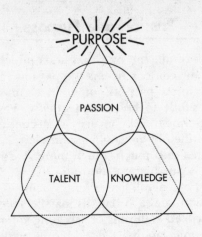

From passion comes purpose, which is at the heart of this book, and vision. This is like mission, only bigger: missions get accomplished but purposes inspire whole lifetimes. If you drew a triangle around the circles representing talent, knowledge, and passion, purpose would be at the apex. Purpose is what the others all lead to, what they are active in response to.

Success Strategy: Aim to Excel. Until you are 40, improve on your weaknesses. After 40, improve on your strengths. Use your awareness of your skills, your knowledge, and your passion to be all that you can be.

Magic

Expect happy surprises from extra effort. Expect magic, like the fortuitous connection with the person you were anxious to meet who appears at a business meeting you almost scrubbed. Or the job that is offered when you make one last call to a prospective employer. Magic is what people mean when they say, "God helps those who help themselves." Magic happens when you heed Eleanor Roosevelt's advice: "You must do the thing you think you cannot do."

As you find yourself, as you discover magic in your life, you will find that there are moments when you forget yourself. There will be times when your work and those you serve so engage your energies that you lose yourself in the moment. What's in here is no longer significant, at that instant, just what's out there.

These are the times when the message transcends the messenger, when the magic transcends the magician; when who we are is subsumed in how we are and what we are offering to the world. We are focused on being, not doing, and our life is a reflection of love.

At the conclusion of a recent workshop I led, the participants all created a life plan like the one described in Chapter 16. They worked on big sheets with bright colors, and on one of the plans I saw a mathematical equation:

Commitment + Love = Magic

When we make up our minds to do something, when we put our whole self behind it, and when we move ahead with caring and compassion, then who knows what kind of unexpected results we will encounter? Commitment plus love equals magic. Not a bad formula. My question to you is: Are you ready for magic in your life?

CHAPTER

14

Right Risks

Nothing venture, nothing gain.

> —Thomas Hardy

It is only by risking our persons from one hour to another that we live at all.

> —William James

Good judgment comes from experience. Experience comes from bad judgment.

> —Thomas Watson

When you bought this book you risked the purchase price. Even if you borrowed it from a library or friend, you risk losing it or forgetting to return it and having to pay a later price. As you read these words your time is at risk, for who knows how much value you will find here? Whatever happens, this book will cost you something.

Your decision to have this book in your hands is reversible. You might return it for a refund or take it back to the person who loaned it to you. No matter how you are feeling about money today, the cost of this experience is probably not a significant item in your personal budget, and will not influence future decisions. Your decision to read these words, like most of the decisions you make, can be reversed. You can recover from it to go on and take new risks.

The only nonreversible decisions are to create life—as a parent—or to take life, your own or someone else's. The following paragraphs are about the other kind of decisions, those that are reversible, a bigger category than most of us realize. These are the big and little risks of day-to-day existence. These are the risks that shape our identity as they refine our sense of purpose.

Kinds of Risks

Decisions are made in the face of three kinds of risks:

1. **Physical Risks:** Even before we are born there are physical risks of the kind reported in medical journals. The moment of birth is physically risky, and the rest of our days each contain some risk, depending on how we live and where we live and what we do. Those who perform stunts for the movies or work as trapeze artists face more physical risks than most of us, but doing any kind of work involves some risk to our physical well-being. The question is how much.

2. **Emotional Risks:** From the beginning of life we take emotional risks. Our first cry is, on some primal level, a call for nurturance; like similar cries throughout our lives, it may not be answered. In our growing-up years the emotional risks become more complex: we risk losing simple games, we risk rejection by our peers, we risk failure in the midterm tests of life. Work is full of emotional risks, starting with our first job application. These risks are essential to success in work and love, and, as William James wrote, essential to keeping us vital.

3. **Resource Risks:** Early on we learn the value of possessions, time, and money. We risk a quarter on a purchase that may disappoint or a dollar on a game our favorite team may lose. These early experiences shape our lifelong attitudes toward risk, our attraction to some risks and fear of others. They explain why some people start businesses and others become their employees. They explain why one woman will go to Belize to serve in the Peace Corps and another to Wall Street to serve investment bankers. Our propensity to take certain kinds of financial risks and avoid others shapes our buying habits, our saving patterns, and our behavior at work. The better we understand our risk-taking style and

the more skillful we become at using it to manage our resources, the richer our lives will become.

Jim, a 39-year-old manager in a consulting firm, knows all about risks. A runner and biker, he takes carefully calculated physical risks: "I always check my bike before starting down the mountain." At his company, Jim is balancing job security with the risk of letting executive search friends know he "might be available" for new challenges. He is confident, energetic, and loyal—yet he suspects there is a better place to commit his considerable passion, a place where he might risk more financially and emotionally but where there is a lot more upside earning and achieving potential.

When you think about what risks are right for you, be like Jim and consider the physical, emotional, and financial. When stuck on a work decision, see if it passes the "feel good" test. What do your instincts tell you? What is your intuitive sense? Then take a moment and write down the risks you see, especially the emotional and financial varieties. Before moving ahead, ask yourself: What is the worst that could happen here? If you can live with those risks, the downside, you are almost ready to act.

Before you do, ask two more questions: What is the worst that could happen if I *don't* take this risk? And: What is the best that will happen to me if I take this risk and it all works out? What we're attracted to tells us as much about right risks as what we avoid.

When invited to give a speech I think of the joys of preparation, the stimulation of attentive faces, the satisfaction of feeling useful. When I am invited by an ad in the newspaper or flier in my mail to make some kind of investment, I usually think of losing money. I prefer the emotional risks of the podium to most financial risks. That's how it is with me, and yet I know people who cringe at the thought of standing before a microphone but love to speculate on the stock market.

It all depends on how we like to work.

Work Styles

In 1891, in a prologue to *Thus Spake Zarathustra*, Friedrich Nietzsche wrote of three metamorphoses of the spirit, "how the spirit becomes a camel; and the camel, a lion; and the lion, finally, a child." The camel, well-loaded, faces challenge and hardship and then, burdened, "speeds into the desert" and becomes a lion "who would conquer his freedom and be master in his own desert." After conquering "Thou Shalt," the preying lion becomes a child of "innocence and forgetting, a new beginning, a game, a self-propelled wheel, a first movement, a sacred 'Yes.' "

You and I are like the camel, the lion, and the child in our work lives, though we might use different names for each phase. My choice—after 12 years of research, lots of structured interviews and lots more informal questioning of career changers, workshop participants, and CEOs—is to call people in these three work-life phases sustainers, venturers, and free spirits.

• *Sustainers* are the bedrock of the world of work: predictable, solid, rarely moving. Sustainers are the consistent performers organizations depend on. Most of us start out as sustainers, passionate about our early work assignments, determined to make our mark somewhere up the hierarchy. At this stage we are usually living out the expectations of our forebears, marching to someone else's drum like loyal camels. We see this as the low-risk path. On the way, we develop skills and accumulate knowledge to shape the success we aspire to. We also develop sustainer values like consistency, loyalty, steadfastness. If we sustain too much, we become unimaginative, unquestioning, and slavish in our devotion to the status quo. What usually happens instead is that we achieve our early goals, grow beyond the sustainer role, and move into a new realm.

As a sustainer, what can you learn about identity and purpose? In the sustainer mode you see yourself as part of the organization you serve and identify with its goals. Your purposes align with its purposes and you may aspire, as I did when I started at Procter & Gamble, to become president. For most of us, however, something happens—we achieve our early goals or find ourselves ejected—and we move into a new realm.

• *Venturers* are more inclined than sustainers to take emotional and financial risks, seeking unique challenges in business, public service, the arts. If sustainers are the bedrock of the world of work, venturers are the rain and the rivers, beating away at tradition, eroding established patterns, and producing continual change. Venturers are entrepreneurs and innovators, converting ideas into enterprises like fearless lions. Most venturers are self-employed or head their own businesses, but some thrive in organizations wise enough to respect their contributions. Venturers are often well into the psychological process Jung called individuation, moving toward what Maslow called self-actualization. Those who become venturers grow more skillful at risk taking while developing self-sufficiency, insight, authenticity, and independence. Someone with too much venturer in them, on the other hand, can be careless, thoughtless, undisciplined, and foolhardy.

How do venturers view purpose? If you are in this mode, your purpose is more individual, more lion-like. Your purpose may be grand and your achievements less so—if you are like me—but at some point you will find yourself growing through the venturer stage to another realm.

• *Free Spirits* move beyond organizational restraints to larger responsibilities, working for whole groups of people or sometimes all the people on the planet. If venturers are the rain and water in the geological metaphor for work-style types, free spirits are the wind and the fire. They beat less on the bedrock of daily existence than venturers, but they exert a far-reaching influence through illumination and inspiration. Free spirits are sometimes employed, with a loose affiliation to an organization, or they may be retired. They take emotional risks—sometimes big ones—but rarely take major financial risks. They sometimes work for money but always for meaning, fulfillment, and joy—in the innocence of new beginnings. Free spirits have dreams but are not dreamers, have ideals without being impractical, and find big challenges to engage the best of their life experience. Free spirits are the counselors, coaches, and mentors you will read about later. You know you are a free spirit when you find yourself pursuing a purpose larger than yourself, but with lightness and joy, taking neither your mission nor yourself too seriously.

Of any 100 people, the great majority will start out as sustainers. Over time, some of these will become venturers and a few of those will move in the world of the free spirit—the spirit of the child. Tracking these people over time produces a pattern that looks something like this:

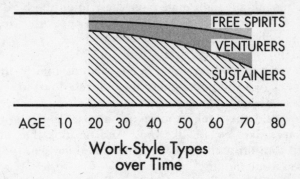

**Work-Style Types
over Time**

To understand what risks are right for you, think about your work style. If you are like most of us, your work involves some combination of styles, with the mix changing as you move from one to another—as you become more of a venturer, say, and less of a sustainer. Wherever you are now, or think you are, you will find value in exploring your risk-taking style.

EXPLORATION: How Do I Take Risks? On a sheet of paper list three headings: PHYSICAL, EMOTIONAL, FINANCIAL. Under each, write the kinds of risks you are willing to take. What risks would you like to take more of? What risks would you like to take less of?

In the Hindu story Joseph Campbell called his favorite, a tigress was about to give birth. She was near starvation because her gestation had made hunting so difficult, but she came upon a herd of goats and was determined to make a kill. Creeping slowly to the top of a small, downwind hill, she poised for her leap. Springing with a roar she fell short, slowed by her weakened muscles and big belly, and died where she landed.

The impact brought on the birth of her cub and when the curious goats returned, they found the helpless critter and nursed him like one of their own. In this way the cub spent his early days, learning to bleat and nibble grass like a goat. His teeth were wrong for grazing, however, and his stomach didn't digest cellulose so he was a miserable-looking specimen.

One morning a giant male tiger came upon the herd and his roar sent the goats scattering. All except the cub, who didn't know enough to be afraid.

"Maaah," said the cub, "who are you?"

"I'm a tiger," said the great beast, carrying him by the scruff of the neck to a still pond where they looked down to see two tiger faces reflected. "And so are you."

"See?" said the tiger. "You're not a goat. You've got a tiger face. You're like me. BE like me!" And he took the cub to his den and tore off a chunk of recently killed gazelle.

"Open your mouth!"

"Oh, no," bleated the cub, "I'm a vegetarian."

But the tiger shoves the raw meat down his throat and the little one gags (as we all do on true doctrine, Campbell adds parenthetically). But the kill is getting into his blood and his tiger nature is awakening. Before long he gives a little stretch and tests his lungs. "Tiger roar 101," Campbell says with a laugh.

"Now you've got it," said the senior tiger. "Now we'll go out into the forest and live like tigers."

The moral of the story, Campbell told us, is that we're all tigers living here as goats. "Live as though you're a goat," Campbell advised, because that is what society demands. But in your inner life, be a tiger. Or, if you've been a sustainer long enough, and are ready for the next step in life, be a lion.

CHAPTER
15
Right Rewards

The quality of Michael Milken's representation will not be affected by Drexel's nickeling and diming their lawyers.

—Arthur Liman, lawyer for Michael Milken, after Drexel Burnham Lambert announced it would pay only $1,250,000 a month for Milken's legal fees.

When I'm up in these hills I feel like the richest man in Taormina.

—Francesco "Chico" Scimone, Sicilian farmer, musician, and world champion race walker who has earned less in his 80 years than Arthur Liman is paid in a month.

"You're going to say Mike and Drexel were greedy, aren't you?" A partner at the now-defunct Drexel Burnham Lambert was concerned with how an interviewer would portray his firm.

"Were you greedy?" the interviewer asked.

"Of course we were, but so were a lot of other people on Wall Street."

Were the rewards—the visibility, the money, the power—worth the price eventually paid? For most of those who worked at Drexel, the answer is no. Even Michael Milken, who accumulated riches that sultans only dream of, would probably agree that the price was too high.

Healthy desires in one are avarice in another, depending on

your perspective. But a billionaire I know puts it this way: "Know what greed is?" he asks. "It's when you pee in the soup." It's healthy to make money, he says—earn your salary, make investments, pursue profitable hobbies—but don't contaminate the source. Don't let avarice spoil the soup.

Sometimes our rewards seem high, sometimes low, for the effort expended. Sometimes what we have seems just right, other times it seems inadequate. Once in a while we are lucky, other times we are not. Most of us come to see some relationship between the risks we take and the rewards that come into our life. Most of us respect the soup.

The intensity with which we apply our talent creates joy, respect, money. If we aspire to happiness in our work and in our lives, we must learn what rewards are right for us.

Rewards Gone Awry

In his rise to power Michael Milken was an idealist, dedicated to helping the underdog by providing money where others would not. He saw an opportunity to offer financing to companies rejected by traditional lenders. He had grand plans and he had a purpose.

But somewhere idealism got twisted by the pursuit of personal rewards, by the glitter of the enormous sums paid to Milken and his followers. Milken lost perspective on the people he was aiming to help. "If you can't make money from your friends," he would say, after taking huge profits from his closest business associates, "who can you make money from?"

That rewards went awry for Michael Milken becomes apparent when the figures are put on paper. From 1983 to 1987 Milken's compensation at Drexel increased twelve-fold, growing more than $500 million in four years.

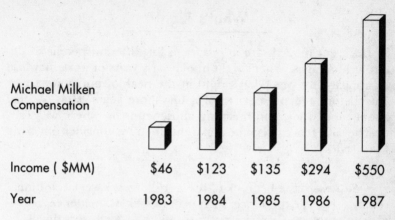

Michael Milken Compensation					
Income ($MM)	$46	$123	$135	$294	$550
Year	1983	1984	1985	1986	1987

This income put Milken beyond the realm of other hardworking and successful people, from heads of giant corporations to heads of state. It put his income ahead of the annual national budgets of most third-world countries.

One indicator of rewards gone awry for Milken was the ever-escalating trend line, with cash compensation heading for the stratosphere. It was growth out of control. In an economic system this is chaos; in the human body it is cancer.

This does not mean that there's anything inherently wrong with money, any more than there's anything wrong with food or water. It's just that too much (or too little) causes problems. Balance is crucial, as a famous economist demonstrated in a major financial decision not long ago. Several New York publishers had bid on the rights to his next two books and when the price got to $2.9 million, he said, "Stop! That's all I'm worth."

Each of us needs to have a sense of what we're worth—how much money, how much respect, how much love. We need to understand the role of rewards in our lives. We need to know what's too much and what's too little and what's just about right.

What's Right?

Different rewards are appropriate for different people at different life stages. What's right in our early years of work may lose its appeal later on. What's right at the peak of our powers may pale before the perspective of a few more years. How we feel about money, joy, and meaning all depends on where we are.

The differences become apparent when we consider our basic work styles:

- *Sustainers,* the bedrock of the world of work, seek traditional rewards. In my experience, such people seek permanence, recognition, adequate financial rewards, and above all, security. They want to know that today's rewards will be there tomorrow and next year. When you are a sustainer, a big part of your reward is seeing the organization prosper and feeling yourself do likewise.

- *Venturers,* those taking the greatest risks, seek rewards that go beyond the traditional. They want money and sometimes reap enormous financial rewards. They want the satisfaction of achievement and are often compulsive in its pursuit. They want reachable challenges, battles to fight where there is a healthy chance of winning. When you are a venturer, reaching for big goals, your rewards can be big—and also your losses.

- *Free Spirits* have usually had security as sustainers and challenges as venturers. These rewards no longer fulfill free spirits, though they continue to want a basic level of security and some healthy challenges in their lives. What draws them forward is meaning, work that makes sense in the world as they view it, work that often makes a profit but always makes a difference.

What links these three types is purpose, an enduring vision of one's life and where it leads. If you see the three work-style types interlinked and at the center of a pyramid, then the apex becomes purpose, the upward thrust that unites the energy of each stage:

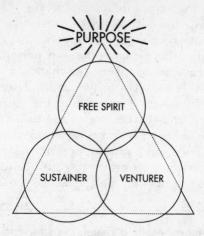

In a typical lifetime, purpose does not change much—jobs come and go, new careers unfold, our vision gets clearer. When I was a college professor, I saw teaching as my purpose in life; today, working with executives and workshop participants, I see myself as a connector. I still teach but the form it takes is linking people with ideas. I'm somewhere between the venturer and free spirit and my primary passion, still, is making work better in the world.

Jim, the 39-year-old consulting firm executive described in the previous chapter, sees himself as a conductor. With a strong background in music and a rich baritone voice, this charismatic leader envisions himself at the head of the orchestra, inspiring the violins, directing the horns, making beautiful music. Though he doesn't talk about it much, his activities at work, on the YMCA board, and in other parts of his life all reflect the passion of a skillful conductor.

Does Jim have it all figured out? No, nor do I. Many of us don't. But I encourage you to continue the search, to continually seek a clearer vision.

Try seeing the quest for purpose like learning soccer. In the beginning we learn the rules. As the game becomes more familiar, we learn the moves. Later on we develop expertise at a particular position or part of the game and our sense of purpose gets clearer. Over time, we play with different teams and different teammates in different uniforms, but the game is the same. Our skills develop and our knowledge grows, but you and I, at core, are the same people we always were.

In soccer and in life, we learn that our personal commitment and plans are important to success but that no one of us controls the outcome. Other players on our team, players on the other team, and the officials all play a role in the outcome, as do the fans, the weather, and the bounce of the ball.

None of this makes our purpose any less important. Our training, dedication, and concentration on the game all make a difference. We continue to strive, we continue to learn, we continue to seek our right place on the field.

Success Strategy: Make It Visual. In soccer and in life, record your goals and your dreams and your progress toward achieving them. Put them on the wall, in colors, where you and those closest to you can see them often. Visual images attract energy. Energy fuels success.

Happiness

G. K. Chesterton knew about right rewards:

When one's interests are concentrated on something bigger than the immediate personal career, upon the social good, upon the larger existence in time and space, upon the cosmic career of the purified soul, it is possible to be eternally, youthfully happy.

Eternal, youthful happiness is an attractive goal, though I have never heard of anyone reaching it. We can concentrate on purposes larger than ourselves, however, and although the rewards may not be eternal, they may be quite satisfying. We may struggle with our desire for Vuarnet sunglasses and Reebok shoes, for a BMW and a big house. We may also long for friendship, family, and time to play. If we remember our purpose, we will know which trade-offs to make and what to risk for which rewards. We will be more likely to keep our perspective.

Recently *The Wall Street Journal* printed a story about perspective and rewards involving a lawyer from Laramie, who wrote to a number of law firms in southern California to help a client collect a $4,240 child-support judgment. No response. Then came a letter from Steve Corris, who must have gone to the same law school as Arthur Liman. "Without sounding pretentious," he wrote, "my retainer for cases is a flat $100,000, with an additional charge of $1,000 per hour."

The lawyer from Laramie, Becky Klemt, responded: "Steve, I've got news—you can't say you charge a $100,000 retainer fee and an additional $1,000 an hour without sounding pretentious. . . . Especially when you're writing to someone in Laramie, Wyoming, where you're considered pretentious if you wear socks to court. . . . Hell, Steve, all the lawyers in Laramie, put together, don't charge $1,000 an hour."

Then she added, "Steve, let us know when we should join you in California so that we can begin doing whatever it is you do. In anticipation of our move, we've all been practicing trying to say we charge $1,000 an hour with a straight face, but so far, we haven't been able to do it. . . .

"P.S. Incidentally, we have advised our client of your hourly rate. She is willing to pay you $1,000 per hour to collect this judgment provided it doesn't take you more than four seconds."

EXPLORATION: What Rewards Are Right for Me? On a sheet of paper write down the rewards you value—things like love, respect, prestige, and money—with as many specifics as you can muster. Put a red star next to the three most important items. Show your list to a friend and ask for reactions and ideas for items you missed.

CHAPTER

16

Big Plans

The superior man is modest in his speech,
but exceeds in his actions.

—Confucius

The function of an ideal is not to be
realized but, like that of the North Star, to
serve as a guiding point.

—Edward Abbey

At Birkenstock we encourage people to
think big. We're working now on our
50-year plan.

—Margot Fraser, CEO

Long ago in a distant land two men set off across a vast desert.
On the third day of the journey a blinding sandstorm swept in
and they became separated. When it was once again possible to
see, neither could find the other. It soon became clear that not
only were they separated, they were lost.

One of the men wandered in circles and before long his water was exhausted. A few steps more and he lay down to die. The
other had less water and less food but he had one thing his lost
companion did not have: he had a map, and because he had a
map he had a plan.

When the surviving traveler finally staggered into an oasis on
the edge of the desert, he discovered that his map was actually of
another desert in another country. With a shock he realized that

a plan, any plan, even one based on the wrong map, is better than no plan at all.

Big Plans

In buying a coat or making a plan, it isn't the size that counts, it's the fit. How big your plans are all depends on how big you want your life to be.

When I was 18 I wanted to be President of the United States and by the time I was 25 I wanted to be president of the Procter & Gamble Company. I had big plans for a big life. How about you? When you think back to your early yearnings do you remember big plans? Notice how even the plans that did not work out have shaped your life.

Consider the stories of three people who had big plans and results they loved—though not the results they planned for.

• As a high school senior, Pat wanted to go the state finals in the half-mile, as her brother had done five years earlier. To stay competitive over the winter she also played on the varsity basketball team and was chosen captain. When track season came around she was undefeated in dual meet competition but missed going to the state meet by one place—while running her best half-mile ever, at 2:08.5. "The next day I got my acceptance to Yale," she says, "and I realized that sports had made the difference. So I missed my goal and got into Yale ... where I expect to be the number one half-miler next year."

• When George went off to Tulane he was reminded in a hundred ways that he was no longer a big frog in a small pond. But he stayed with his big plan—to become president of the student association—and forged many important alliances in his new larger pond. He missed his goal but was twice elected to class offices which, he is sure, helped him get into law school. "Having a big goal served me well," he says now. "I have absolutely no regrets."

• Chris was ecstatic when she was accepted at the Harvard Business School, as her father had been 25 years earlier. But she was surprised when good grades proved much more elusive than at the liberal arts college where she had done her undergraduate work. She missed her goal of being in the top third of the class, but says, "Having that goal gave me the focus I needed to keep going through a tedious, back-breaking work load." Five years later, nobody cares about her grades, and she thrives in a high-pressure job at Morgan Stanley.

Pat, George, and Chris talked about their big plans with close friends and key allies. This gave them feedback, support, respect—and insight into an important strategy for success:

Success Strategy: Share Your Dreams. The more near-term your goal the more value you will find in telling others about it. You strengthen your commitment even more by setting a target date. We all need help for our dreams to come true.

As I write these words, I am looking at a yellowed copy of *The New York Times* best-seller list on which number ⑦ has three big circles around it and FINDING THE HAT THAT FITS written beside it. Whether or not that goal is achieved, whether or not my big plan comes true, my expectation is that this book will bring information and inspiration to many, including you.

"Write a best-seller" was a goal I set during a seminar in the fall of 1988. The homework was to conceive of an unthinkable accomplishment and that seemed unthinkable enough. We told others in the seminar of our goal and I still remember the flutters in my belly as I said, "Write a best-seller by 1992" and how good I felt a moment later.

Does *The New York Times* list on my wall make a difference? When I was sketching the outline for this book, I kept thinking, "This has got to be good." When I'm searching for the right word, and I remember the faces in that seminar, I take an extra minute and look in my dictionary to get it right. When the idea I'm trying to express is fuzzy, I pause to search for clarity. When I smell cliché, I try for something more original. In refining and revising, I ask professional and literary critics to comment on these words.

The aging newspaper page on my wall makes a difference. For me, writing a best-seller is a big, big plan and I intend to do my part in making it possible. This is a team game, like soccer, and I do not control the final outcome. But I do control my actions and my plan, which I tell you about here to inspire you to think bigger. There are people who think too big, who aim too high, but I don't know many. Most of us think too small. We think that we can't have what we want and if we try for it the result will only be disappointment. My hope is that you will not sell yourself short. My hope is that you will create a plan for yourself just a bit bigger than your potential to achieve it, and that the result of your courageousness in setting that goal will be wonderful surprises in your life.

Life Plans

My plan includes more than work and professional accomplishment. Yours should, too. Besides work—the big and little accomplishments to which we commit our energies—there are three other pieces to any life plan:

• **Play** belongs in every healthy life. What are you doing for fun? How do you revitalize your spiritual and physical energies? Your plan can include sports and exercise. It can include games, indoors or out. It can include travel, near or far. It should include learning something new, which leads into the next aspect of life planning.

• **Learning** is part of every healthy life, and it goes on as long as we draw breath. As you plan, think about what classes, seminars, and workshops you want to take. What new skills will you learn? What knowledge will you add to the huge amount already stored in your brain? Is part of your dream to earn a degree? Including it in your plan will help it come true.

• **Love** is the fourth part of a life plan. *"Lieben und arbeiten,"* Freud answered when asked what the normal person should be capable of: "To love and to work." What do you want in the relational part of your life? More closeness with family or friends? New friends or lovers? A spouse? Children?

Can you see how one could have "unthinkable accomplishments" in any one of these realms? Learning to speak Mandarin could be one and climbing Mount Kilimanjaro another. Whatever we call it—impossible dream, lifelong ambition, vision—it is important for each of us to think carefully about what it is we want most in our life.

One way to do it is with an exercise I've used in career-change workshops since 1983. Start with colored markers, pastels, crayons, and a large sheet of paper, as big as 27 by 32 inches, or as small as you're willing for your life to be. In the center of the paper draw a dot the size of a dime. That dime is time present and everything else is the future, working out as far as you want. The top of the sheet will include your plans for work, the right-hand side for play, the left-hand side for learning, and the bottom for love. Your layout will look like this:

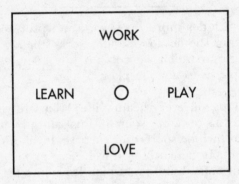

You can draw pictures on your sheet, if you promise not to make this a test of your artistic skills; you can write words and even make lists. You can take as long as necessary, though most people need only 45 minutes. If you drew a picture of your life as part of Step One in the first chapter, you can look at it again for new ideas. Take insight wherever you find it.

This is your plan, and you can make it whatever you want. You can also use it any way you want, but I hope you'll use it like a man I spoke with recently, who said: "Three years after your workshop, John, I still have my life plan taped to my wall. I've added to it, but I'm still pursuing goals I committed to then."

> **Success Strategy: Develop Your Own Best Planning Process.** We all make plans in our head, but successful people go beyond that—to typewritten plans, to pictures with words, to symbols and icons, to honors and awards. Try different combinations until you have an approach that works for you.

Action Steps

On your life plan you can add specific action steps under WORK, PLAY, LEARN, and LOVE. Specific action steps are the little things we do to make things happen, like "Print my résumé by 3/14" or "Call Paul by 4/1." They can also represent an accumulation of little steps: For instance, the goal "Sell my car by 7/1" involves placing ads, waxing the car, phoning friends, meeting prospects, negotiating a price, and completing the paperwork.

You can see this as a pyramid of plans, with your big goals and dreams at the top, the mid-level plans just below, and at the bottom all the little pieces that are the foundation for the whole thing. If you yearned to be an airline pilot, like 23-year-old Tad, your plans would look like this:

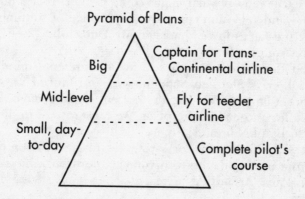

Pyramid of Plans

Big — Captain for Trans-Continental airline

Mid-level — Fly for feeder airline

Small, day-to-day — Complete pilot's course

For the middle-size steps and also for the small ones on your daily "To Do" list, it is important to acknowledge your own progress. One of the best ways to do this is to cross off each item when it is accomplished. I use an orange marker for its visual impact. It's even okay to add an item to the list *after* you've done it and cross it off as a small celebration of your accomplishment. I know an editor who starts his "To Do" list with "Make List" to give himself a running start. When the list is done he has already completed the first task.

In making your plans it's essential to remember that none of this is done in a vacuum. All of us are interconnected and all of us need help in making our dreams come true. Include this reality in your plans. Include the people to whom you will reach out as you make your plans come true.

You Must Be Present

In the good old days we'd buy a raffle ticket to support the local soccer team and after hearing about the prizes and paying our dollar, we'd see printed on the ticket the words "You must be present to win." For most raffles these days you need not be present to win, and that's how a lot of people live their lives. They are not really here and even when their physical bodies are in the room their minds are on the frustrations of getting here or the excitement of what might come next. They are not really present—and they don't stand much chance of winning. They are like the James Joyce character, Mr. Duffy, who "lived a short distance from his body."

Good things come to those who are present—mind, body, and soul—says Stephen Schoen, who introduced me to this raffle-ticket imagery. We must be present in the game of life. We must be here to collect the prize. We must say yes to life's invitation to be present and win.

There are four steps for saying yes to life in your meeting tomorrow, in negotiating with your landlord, in achieving your biggest plans. According to real-estate executive Susan Melvin, these are:

1. Show up.
2. Listen well.
3. Speak the truth.
4. Stay open to all possibilities.

These require alertness, practice, and patience. But if you follow these four simple steps you will get what you want in life . . . or at least what you need.

EXPLORATION: Where Do I Go from Here? What do I want most in work? in play? in learning? in relationships? Draw a life plan reflecting work, play, learning, and love. Be willing to make a big plan. Be present. Be prepared to win.

All we can do is stay true to our dreams and work at our plans. Like the man finding his way across the desert, we must move forward confident of arriving at the right place.

At the same time, no matter how skillfully we plan, the future is never fully within our control. There are complications from sea changes, sandstorms, luck, and fate. There are actions by other people we never anticipated, and gifts from the universe to bless our journey. Still, the lesson of the story holds: *Any* plan will make the trip better. Big plans and focused actions will produce astonishing results.

17

The Power of Promises

DEAR ABBY: What is the difference
between saying you will do something
and promising to do it?

Muncie, Ind.

DEAR MUNCIE: If the person's word is
good, there is no difference.

The promise made to you, faithful reader, at the start of this
book was that you would be taken through seven steps to finding
your purpose in life and be shown a map for living it, complete
with travel tips. You've seen the map, with seven spots visited on
the journey, and you've gotten some ideas for making the trip a
happy one. So far, so good.

What holds all this together is promises, like those made in
the first pages you read. Promises are the link between ideas and
planning, and then between planning and action. Promises are
what move us toward our vision as we traverse the territory described by the career cycle map. Promises are the linchpins of
life: they separate progress from chaos.

Promises on the Road

At every stage in the journey there are opportunities to raise
our level of commitment by giving our word. At every stage there
are prerequisites that must be fulfilled by giving our word. Without making promises, big and small, we do not move ahead.

Early in our life we learn about promises made to other people, promises to sweep the porch or to be home by dark. These are important. As we taste more of life we learn about promises made to ourselves, about things we will do or not do, about ways we want to be. These are the most powerful of all promises—those made of our own volition for our own benefit and witnessed by other people. That is when our word has the greatest power.

Promises power us around the career cycle. These are the commitments that keep us rolling:

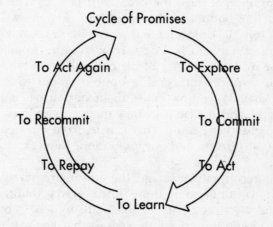

Cycle of Promises

To Act Again   To Explore

To Recommit   To Commit

To Repay   To Act

To Learn

While there are many small promises at each stage, each stage has its primary promise without which there can be no progress.

• At the discontent stage on the cycle, the promise is *to explore*. Many people are slowed down here; a few stop altogether. What life is asking is that we develop options for handling discontent. What happens when we decide to explore is that we see new possibilities and begin to move.

• At the exploration stage on the cycle, the promise is *to commit*, to select one option out of many and say yes to it. Some people explore forever without committing to act on what they discover. Skillful wayfarers are continually exploring and ready to commit when enough data are in and the time is right. They know that small commitments lead to larger ones.

• At the commitment stage, the promise is *to act*. Commitment is the green light; acting is the foot on the gas pedal. Commitment is the earth-moving idea; acting is all the little things to be done, a shovelful at a time. These small acts aggregate into the big actions that carry us through the bottom of the cycle.

• At the change point the promise is *to learn*. Some people live and learn, my father used to say, others just live. Aspire to learn, especially at the bottom of the cycle, when difficult—and valuable—lessons are offered to us by our life experience.

• At the renewal stage the promise is *to repay*. The boon carried out of the bottom of the cycle must be delivered to those ready to receive it. Unless there is a promise to repay, an internal recognition of a gift to be given, renewal is not complete.

• At the integration stage of the cycle, the promise is *to recommit*, which requires impeccable honesty about what we have learned. What do we now know about our virtues and defects, our strengths and deficiencies now that we have come through the dark night of the soul? What is true, from this new perspective, about our dreams and our motivation? Remember, reality always wins.

• At the recommitment stage, the promise required of us is *to act again*, to continue to do those little everyday things that keep us alive and alert on a journey that will surely be repeated. We are called to continue the little actions that keep us moving at each point on the cycle. We are called to continue to repay, to be honest, to explore.

As we travel the paths through work and life we find many opportunities to make promises, to give our word to ourselves and others. How we do this, and when, determines the quality of the journey.

Promises and Reality

Between possibility and reality lies the promise. The difference between what might happen and what actually happens is someone making the commitment and giving their word. Commitments are supported by energy, money, and time.

There is physical energy, like that used to clear a field, and there is the mental energy that solves financial problems. There is also psychic energy that inspires individuals and stimulates groups.

Money is energy on paper: the kind that goes in your wallet or the kind that appears on checks, bank statements, loan documents, invoices, and purchase orders. Money is less important than most of us think and more available than most of us imagine. When we remember our plan and are true to our purpose, there is enough money—though the amount and the timing of its arrival may not be what we expected.

What's really limited in availability is time, the little pieces of time that add up to the big pieces required to make anything important happen. Time is irreplaceable, unbankable, and distributed equally to everyone, regardless of how clever or educated or wealthy we are.

Promises usually involve time, and the amount dictates the quality of the promise. Promises requiring several years to fulfill are less predictable, less manageable, and less precise than those requiring a few minutes. If we promise to make a phone call this afternoon, we can be fairly sure of keeping our word, whereas a promise to save enough to buy a house requires more commitment. The relationship between time and commitment looks like this:

- Commitment to TASKS is short term: hours, days, weeks
- Commitment to OBJECTIVES is mid term: 6 to 36 months
- Commitment to MISSIONS is long term: 2 to 5 years
- Commitment to PURPOSES is long, too: 10 to 15 years

Success Strategy: Make More Promises. Resist the impulse to make fewer promises and make more—when they align with your purpose and lead to your vision. Otherwise, like Nancy Reagan, just say no.

Promises to Whom?

The early promises we make to parents and to ourselves prepare us for making commitments as adults. This is important training: Promises kept to prospective employers, to co-workers, and to supervisors are crucial to success in the world of work.

The most important promises join groups of people in productive activities. These promises are how countries get created and great projects completed, how companies grow and space vehicles go into orbit. These are the agreements that change the way we see our world—like the promises made by, to, and among six adventurers who recently became the first persons to cross Antarctica on foot.

On March 3, 1990, these adventurers hailing from China, France, Great Britain, Japan, the Soviet Union, and the United States completed a 3,740-mile ski trek across the continent at the bottom of the world. Amazing? "Everything looks impossible for the people who never try anything," according to the expedition's co-leader, a French physician. Everything looks impossible for those people who never promise anything, too.

"Of course I had doubts that we could do it," said the expedition's British navigator. "But I never let them enter my conscious mind. You have to throw the doubt out of your mind."

It's okay for those of us who commit to smaller challenges to have doubts, too. We, like the six skiers, might fail at what we attempt. What's not okay is to fail to try at all.

Promises empower. Whether it is a trek across Antarctica or a trip to sign up a new client, our promise to do the thing vastly increases our chance of success. This does not mean that it's easy to make promises or that we all make them in the same way: some people are better with promises about time than with those about money or can easily make promises to themselves but find making them to other people more difficult. Some people have trouble making promises at all. Whatever your style, remember that what works for Antarctic explorers—proceeding as if you had no doubts—can work for you, too.

EXPLORATION: What Promises Shape My Life? What promises to myself? What promises to others? What promises about work? What promises about relationships? What changes could I make to have a happier, more purposeful life?

This book is about moving ahead in life, about making the right moves at the right time. Such forward motion is complex, and none of it happens without commitment. Wherever there is activity there will be promises, by someone to someone, powering the progress.

18

Lady Luck

Let your hook always be cast; in the
stream when you least expect it, there will
be a fish.

—Ovid

Be like the cowbird. The cowbird eats
through the dung to get to the kernels. Be
disciplined enough to plow through the
manure to get to the gold.

—CEO, major bank

Lady luck was sitting on my shoulder the day I walked into my
tent in the Mendocino woods and met Manny Talkovsky. Casual
and bearded, eight years my senior, Manny's blue eyes sparkle
with intelligence and wit.

We were among 80 men who attended a Robert Bly retreat on
the northern California coast—eight days filled with poetry and
magic, laughter and synchronicity. Bly is full of bluster and balo-
ney, strong opinions, wise words, and deep affections—and I was
delighted to know him better. But best of all was Manny.

Manny and I were tent-mates during those eight days and became good friends. My wife and I like to visit the coast, near the
area where Manny and his wife live, and soon the friendship became four-way. When I ended a 10-year academic career a few
months later, partly so my wife and I could take an extended sabbatical, it was Manny who told us to extend a trip we'd planned,
saying "Stay nine months—anything less is just a vacation."

Those nine months in Europe were a treasured time in the

life and love I share with my wife—for which I have thanked
Manny many times in many ways. "Lucky I got to know you," I
said at the time, but the best was yet to come.

As we talked about our lives Manny told me of expanding his
printing company and then selling it with the help of other
CEOs in a group called TEC. Weird name, I thought. This low-
tech guy is more interested in people than technology.

TEC, Manny explained, is an acronym for "The Executive
Committee." When he told me how it organized CEOs into ongoing groups of 12, I was intrigued. "Each group is led by a
chairman," Manny told me. "He's the organizer, the facilitator,
the spark plug." There are more than 200 TEC groups in this
country and abroad, I discovered. They meet monthly, 12 or 14
CEOs, to spend three hours with a business expert and then, in
the afternoon, to help one another solve problems. Between
meetings the chairman spends two hours one-on-one with each
member, listening and asking questions.

Working with CEOs appealed to me. I had been calling them
for consulting jobs, without much success, and I had less work
than I wanted—and some professional loneliness. I had lost
momentum while abroad, it seemed. My new career, which was
supposed to take off like a rocket, was taking off like a rock instead. So I called San Diego, where The Executive Committee is
based, and discovered they were looking for a chairman in my
area. Three months and several interviews later, I signed a con-
tract as an independent contractor to start my own TEC group.
Exploration led to commitment and a change in my life.

It was an exciting moment, but it would have been even more
exciting if I had known then what I know now. If I had known
the satisfaction I would get from recruiting men and women into
the group, the rewards of solving problems with them, the pleasure of intimacy with people I admire—if I had known how fulfilling the work would be, my joy on signing would have been
uncontainable.

As someone who preaches planning I was surprised when the
joy of working with my CEO group exceeded not only my expectations but also my hopes. What I had missed in setting goals in
1987 was the human factor, the value I get from working closely

with people I like. As a result, my work today rates 12 on a scale of 10, 20 percent *above* my best-case plan—a fortuitous misjudgment I wish for you too.

Not long ago, I was discussing life purpose with a member of my TEC group, Jason Gilman, as we visited five record stores in the chain he was managing. He is searching for his purpose, his vision, for a transcendent idea to inspire his life and his company. "I can see your purpose reflected in our group, John. Connecting people and ideas works for us." He sighed. "I just wish it could work that well for me."

I wish you luck, Jason, with your stores and with your life, like the luck we have had in our TEC group. We will help you, Jason, as you have helped others, and others have helped us. We will do all we can, Jason, to help you get lucky.

Getting Lucky

Jason Gilman has already had lots of luck, in Las Vegas casinos and betting on football games. But the luck we are talking about here is different. This luck is available to each of us, whether we like to gamble or not. This luck comes from getting ourselves to the right place at the right time, from continually learning, and from adopting the attitudes that invite good fortune. The five most important of these attitudes are:

• *Optimism.* All of the successful people I have studied, especially as part of my doctoral research in the early 1980s, are optimists. Definitely not Pollyannas, but *tough-minded* optimists. They believe their goals can be accomplished. They have confidence and faith, sometimes even serenity. Like the tough-minded optimists described by Alan McGinnis in *The Power of Optimism,* they . . .

- are seldom surprised by problems
- look for partial solutions
- believe they have control over their future
- allow for regular renewal

- interrupt their negative trains of thought
- heighten their powers of appreciation
- use their imagination to rehearse success
- are cheerful even when they can't be happy
- have a high capacity for stretching
- build lots of love into their lives
- like to swap good news
- accept what cannot be changed

- *Inquisitiveness.* Lucky people are interested, curious, inquisitive. They have open eyes, open ears, open minds. They take positions and make decisions, but they also cultivate the "don't know mind" as taught by the Buddhists. One of the best listeners I know is Jason Gilman, a man who is always asking questions.
- *Persistence.* Lucky people, successful people persevere. They try once, twice, a third time. They try new ways, using new ideas, knocking on new doors, speaking to new people. But they also remember the advice of W. C. Fields: "If at first you don't succeed, try, try again. Then quit. There's no use being a damn fool about it."
- *Tolerance.* Fortunate people are tolerant of their own shortcomings and of those they recognize in others. They accept diversity into their lives and are receptive to new ideas. They are slow to judge and quick to praise.
- *Gratitude.* McGinnis affirms "powers of appreciation" and Roberto Assigioli, the father of psychosynthesis, speaks of an "attitude of gratitude," which he sees as the highest state a person can achieve. Lucky people take time to feel grateful—at the end of the day, the week, the year. They give thanks for blessings received—and not received. They regularly thank those around them with words, gestures, gifts, momentos, and celebrations.

Success Strategy: Hang In There. Give luck a chance to work for you. "The secret of life," Jason Gilman likes to say, "is to hang around long enough to get lucky."

Bodies in Motion

"Activity of any kind," writes Lynne Cheney, "no matter how unfocused and random, seems to stir the water and cause things to happen." In a 1986 article on how famous people got their big breaks, Cheney quoted neurologist James Austin, who says, "Chance favors those in motion."

Bodies in motion—whether they are heavenly bodies or earthly bodies made of flesh and blood—have a better chance of ending up where the action is than their stay-at-home counterparts. Successful people, the ones others call lucky, are always active. They stay close to old friends and make new ones. They attend seminars, workshops, speeches, conventions, trade shows, and book signings. They ask questions, explore possibilities, test options, and try new restaurants. They have balance in their lives and remember to rest, but they are bodies in motion.

I have seen these traits in hundreds of successful people, this has been my experience, and this is my advice to you: Don't wait for Lady Luck to visit—go out and meet her.

Bring good fortune into your life by using the secrets of successful people. Follow the seven laws of luck:

1. **Luck comes more to some people than to others.** Unlike luck at bingo, good fortune in life is not random.
2. **Luck comes to those who learn it.** Good fortune comes from learning about luck, through example and experience, and then acting upon that knowledge.
3. **Luck comes in waves.** Like skillful surfers, lucky people know how to ride the good waves.
4. **Attitude influences luck.** Lucky people are optimistic, inquisitive, persistent, tolerant, and grateful.
5. **Purpose influences luck.** Purposes that are conscious, congruent, and clearly communicated draw good fortune like flowers draw hummingbirds.
6. **Luck loves the active.** The more active we are when we know what we want, the more likely we are to get it.
7. **Luck comes to those who are doing the right work.** Not only do we find the joy that comes from the proper use of

our talent and passion, we also find good fortune in our lives.

Luck, which lots of people talk about, is something all of us can create. All of us can do something each day to bring more luck into our lives and the lives of those around us. The steps aren't that difficult. We just need to take them.

We need to remember our vision—like Lily Tomlin, who says, "When I was growing up, I really wanted to be somebody. Now I realize I should have been more specific." Or Yogi Berra, who says, "If you don't know where you're going, you're liable to end up somewhere else." Or newspaperman Steve McNamara, who says, "If you want to catch fish, you have to go fishing."

EXPLORATION: How Can I Improve My Luck? Look at your plans—the visual versions, those in words, those in your head—and see how you can use the Seven Laws of Luck to help these plans bear more fruit.

PART

IV

Making Progress

CHAPTER

19

Do What You Love, Love What You Do

Love is all there is . . .

—Emily Dickinson

When we encounter the spiritual passion of Desire with a big D we are corralling all our resources—intellectual, emotional, physical, imaginative, the animal and the angelic—and pouring them into our work.

—Stephen Nachmanovitch, teacher and author

A man without passion would be like a body without a soul. Or even more grotesque, like a soul without a body.

—Edward Abbey

Could you weave a carpet "more beautiful than the eyes of man had ever yet beheld"? A carpet with lilies and roses and brightly colored birds lacking "nothing but the gift of song"? A young maiden in one of the Grimms' Fairy Tales could because, as the story makes clear, she was doing what she loved.

This young woman was poor but prolific in her spinning, weaving, and sewing. "It seemed as if the flax in her room increased of its own accord," the story tells us, "and whenever she wove a piece of cloth or carpet, or made a shirt, she at once found a buyer who paid her amply for it, so that she was in want of nothing, and even had something to share with others."

Like many of the Grimms' stories, this one ends happily, when the maiden is discovered by a king's son who has proclaimed, "She shall be my wife who is the poorest, and at the same time the richest." While she lived simply in a humble cottage this young woman had become rich in the fiber arts that engaged her creative spirit. Her match with the king's son was perfect.

Few things are as satisfying, or as productive of wonderful results, as being totally engaged with our purpose—in a fairy tale or in earning our daily bread.

Dick Bolles, who has devoted lots of love and years of work to *What Color Is Your Parachute?* expressed this in the form of a question: "Remember the last time you were so engrossed in what you were doing that you lost track of time?" Bolles went on to tell the group to whom he was speaking, "Whatever you are doing then you should be doing more of as part of your daily work." Another way to find work you love, he said, is to make a list of people you admire and see what they are doing. Or ask yourself which skills you most enjoy using. "You are good at what you enjoy," Bolles told his listeners, "with the possible exceptions of golf and tennis." At the end, Bolles told us that "the problem for a lot of people is that they are looking for half their vision with half their guts."

If we truly aspire to do work that we love, it is incumbent upon us to lift up our eyes and seek out a whole vision. Then we must look for the right work with all our heart, soul, and energy. This is not always easy.

We may go through stages when our choices are limited and our work is not enough or not right. We may feel compromised and confused. We may be discouraged, disoriented, and disinclined to do what is required to get on the right track. We may be deeply discontented, and unsure how to move through that part of the cycle. We can survive these times, and thrive on what we have learned, if we persevere in pursuit of our dream.

Do What You Love

In all the counseling I have done and workshops I have led, from all the listeners I have spoken with on call-in shows, I have heard one lament more than any other: "I don't know what work I want to do." Even the most successful and richly employed people struggle with this question at one time or another. In the search for the answer a good place to start is with the approaches suggested by Dick Bolles:

• **What were you doing when you last lost track of time?** What activities engage you so completely that nothing else seems to matter? Mihaly Csikszentmihalyi, a psychologist at the University of Chicago, calls this "flow," a state of concentration that amounts to absolute absorption in an activity. It's when we have "a feeling of creative discovery, a challenge overcome, a difficulty resolved." When you have this feeling, see what it comes from and see if you can get more of it into your work.

• **Whom do you admire?** Make a list of those who hold your attention, those you envy, people you emulate, people who engage your imagination. Who would be in your Hall of Fame for living lives you respect? Who are the lifetime members? What do you admire about their lives and their accomplishments? How can you find similar accomplishments in your own life? The more your work is dedicated to accomplishments about which you are passionate, the more likely it is to be work you love.

• **What skills do you enjoy using?** Every job-finding book ever written asks this question in one form or another, and with good reason. There is a high correlation between what we enjoy and what we are good at. Skills are what we can do, the big things and the little things. The more we know about our skills the more likely we are to make intelligent job choices. If we are doing what we are good at, there is a good chance we will be doing work we love.

• **What work have you loved in the past?** A good summing-up exercise is to scan your work history and see which period gave you the most joy. Start by thinking about challenges met, about difficulties mastered. What about those times did you like? How can you bring more of this into your present work? You can take parts of former jobs or conditions that brought great happiness and re-create them to make your work more appealing this week, this month, this year.

• **What work do you think you would love to do in the future?** This final summing-up question asks you to trust your intuition, to honor the value of your wishes and the power of your dreams. John Holland wrote that "the most efficient way to predict vocational choice is simply to ask the person what he wants to be; our best devices do not exceed the predictive value of that method." A pioneer in the field of helping people find the right work, Holland's observation was based on years of research—and a reverence for human instinct.

You will recognize in these questions several of the steps to finding your purpose in life—which is natural, because purpose and work are pieces of the same life fabric. Finding work we love is a major, ongoing task. But it only takes us partway to where we want to go.

Love What You Do

In fairy tales and in life, even the most perfect work has moments of unpleasantness, discomfort, and discouragement. Even the best job requires some compromise between what we want and what someone else wants, between what we believe and the reality around us. No matter what we are doing, there will be mornings when work seems less than perfect, afternoons when we are bored, and evenings when we wish we were doing something a little—or even a lot—different.

There is no perfect job, just as there is no perfect friend or perfect spouse or perfect automobile. We can find jobs we love, just as we can find friends and spouses and cars we love, but there is always some accommodation required.

In work some of the most significant accommodation involves people, places, time, and money:

• **People** can be a problem, even when you love your work, if there are too many or too few or even one or two who grate on your tender spots. When this happens, keep the work and change the people—as much as possible. Seek a different relationship with your boss or co-worker. Change jobs or even employers. Do the work where there are fewer people (or more) or more compatible personalities. Work we love is not static, but a moving target, and the motion usually includes some change in the cast of characters.

• **Places** are a problem if they are too far away or too hot or too dirty or too crowded. If you are doing work you love but it is in the wrong part of town or in the wrong part of the world, then you need to change either the place or the way you view it. One way to find work you love is to ask yourself where you want to work. In the city or in the country? In a big operation or a small one? In your home or in an office? One way to maintain the quality of work is to improve upon the place, to move closer to perfect. Ask yourself: how important is *where* I work compared to *with whom* and *at what*? Look for ways to change what is most important to you.

• **Time** is a problem if your work interferes with healthy relationships with family and friends, from the exercise you need to feel good, and from the moments of spiritual renewal essential to human happiness. If you are doing work you love, there may be days or even weeks when that work demands more hours than you would like to give. If you want to continue loving that work, though, you need to find ways to balance your dedication to it with other passions in your life.

• **Money** is another facet of the time problem. If you could do work you love for fewer hours per week, would you be willing to take less money? A Time Values Survey conducted by Hilton Hotels found that 70 percent of those earning $30,000 a year or more would give up a day's pay for an extra day of free time. How about you? Money can't buy love, at work or anywhere else. But without a little money and the essentials for living it is difficult to think about love at all. Ask yourself: How much money do I want? How much money do I need? How does the difference between those two figures affect my chances for finding work that I love?

Success Strategy: Prepare a personal plan each December. Include in your plan people, places, time, money—and what you want in each category, as well as changes you want to make. Include your purpose, missions, objectives, and goals. Review the plan every six months and make adjustments.

If you and I aspire to love what we do, we must be observant of the great cycles of work in our lives. In periods of renewal following major change, it is natural to love what we do. But as we move into periods of integration it is useful to note what is good about our work and find ways to include more of it in our lives. We know that there will be times of discontent ahead and we can prepare for them by learning, and acting upon what we learn, at every stage in the cycle. We can become, as the Spanish say, an "explorador."

"Do What You Love, the Money Will Follow is my acknowledgment," says author Marsha Sinetar, "to all people who do the work they really enjoy." The subtitle for her book is "Discovering Your Right Livelihood." Wouldn't you like to do that?

EXPLORATION: What Work Do I Love? How does your work rate today on a 10-point scale? What would it take to get you to better than perfect, say a 12? How can you find work that will give you that much bliss? Start today to make it happen.

Whatever work you do, look for ways to discover more value in each day. Listen for the whisper of the big D—Desire—and look for ways to respond. Remember the words of Oliver Wendell Holmes:

As life is action and passion, it is required that we should share the passion of our time at the peril of being judged not to have lived.

CHAPTER

20

Objectives over Obstacles

> Many things, having full reference
> To one consent, may work contrariously;
> As many arrows, loosed several ways,
> Fly to one mark; as many ways meet in
>   one town;
> As many streams meet in one salt sea;
> As many lines close in the dial's center;
> So may a thousand actions, once afoot,
> End in one purpose, and be all well borne
> Without defeat.
>
> —Shakespeare

> When the situation is desperate, it is too
> late to be serious. Try playfulness.
>
> —Edward Abbey

The Right Reverend William E. Swing, a man who has found great success in life, is a big fan of failure.

Now Episcopal Bishop of California, Swing likes to tell a story about his college days. "I was given an honorary doctorate from Kenyon College, along with two other men," he told me, "and the night before the ceremony I asked the others how they had done at Kenyon, because I was such a lousy student and my track record was so embarrassing that I didn't feel right about going out on that platform to receive that degree.

" 'How about you guys?' I asked. One was the head of the Peace Corps and he said, 'I didn't last one year at Kenyon.' The other was Jonathan Winters, the comedian, and he said, 'Oh, they kicked me out by February.'

"And I said, 'They asked me to leave by the end of my sophomore year.' And we asked ourselves why the three dummies sitting around this table, of all the people who go to Kenyon, were the ones invited back to be given honorary degrees."

And?

"Two things came out of that. One was that we learned failure by age twenty. Some people don't learn what failure is about until they're forty-five, and then they can't handle it. If you can fail in front of your peers and God and everybody and discover that life goes on, then you are ready for marriage, you're ready for raising children, you're ready for a career. If you really understand that there's life after failure, then you're in good shape. How lucky we were to fail early!

"The second thing," Swing says with a smile, "was how fortunate it is to discover early on in life what your passion is about in the world and spend your life firsthand working on your passion rather than second or third hand working at somebody else's passion."

Passion

Life works best when our energies are passionately engaged, when our work is inspired by deep desires. Vocational counselors test for interests, but passions and deep desires are bigger. They involve a lot of interests together and where they lead. Nothing moves us like passion.

In my experience, no one—not students and not corporate presidents—understands their passion with perfect clarity. After all, passion is about feeling, not about thinking. But it can be brought into focus and one useful image for doing this is a target, like the archer aims for, with a bull's-eye in the center.

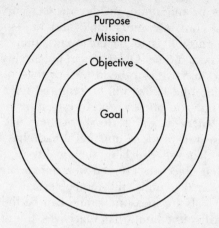

In this imagery, the expanding rings in the target represent bigger and bigger ideas set in longer and longer time frames. The total picture is the vision that draws your energy and keeps your passion stoked. It works best if you start with the largest ring and move inward.

• **Purpose** is the biggie, what your life is all about. This may change, or your perception of it may change, every 10 or 15 years. In business, as Jim Collins and Jerry Porras at the Stanford Business School point out, "the single most crucial factor in the success of any organizational effort is a clear and powerful over-all aim." The same is true for individuals. Don wants to save the rain forests in the Amazon River Basin, a purpose that will prob-ably inspire him to leave a secure job at Safeway Stores. How about you? Where are you being drawn?

• **Mission** is the major activity, or maybe two or three major activities, now engaging your passion in pursuit of your purpose. We are not talking about Mission Impossible here, but we are talking about a major two- to five-year effort. For Don, a core mission is to travel to Brazil to photograph the beauty and the destruction of the rain forests there. He knows it won't be easy to find the money, time, and opportunity—but he is committed. How about your missions? What major efforts are engaging your energies at this point in your life?

• **Objectives** are milestones on the way to completing missions and, unlike missions, are measurable and time-specific. It's like soccer: if your mission is to be champion, then your objectives come one victory at a time. Objectives in life are just as important. For Don, a key objective is to build his portfolio of nature photographs to the level he knows will be required for an invitation to Brazil. He can envision photos from forests in his native California and he knows where he will go to shoot them. He can see the 8 × 10 glossies he will produce and he already has the handsome leather folder that will proclaim the quality of his work. How about you? What objectives are you working toward today?

• **Goals** are smaller units still, mini-objectives that lead to bigger successes. Goals are measurable and can be the smallest tasks. They have specific time limits, like objectives, but are measured in smaller increments and shorter time periods. As in soccer, goals lead to victory. One of Don's goals right now is to visit Yosemite when the spring flowers are blooming. He plans to go next weekend and, when he goes, it will be one more arrow in the center of the target, one small step toward saving the rain forests.

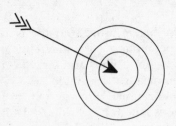

Can you fill in the blanks?

	Don	You
Purpose (1)	Save Rain Forests	
Mission (2–3)	Photograph Amazon	
Objective (3–5)	Build Portfolio	
Goal (5–10)	Visit Yosemite	

Why is all this so important? For one thing, in an age when the average supermarket has 25,000 items to pick from, when there are 11,000 magazines we can buy, and more than 50 TV channels to select from, having a purpose makes decisions easier. For another thing, it's exciting to hit our goals. It's a joy to be living on purpose.

Purposes Past

The most important mission in my life today is this book. But when I was just out of school my mission was to become the president of the Procter & Gamble Company. No matter that I was a new hire, naive, and neurotic, I knew what I wanted.

Part of achieving this goal, as I saw it, was flashy success at every step on my inevitable rise up the corporate ladder. The second step for me, after a year in product management, was a sales training assignment in Connecticut. When a Thanksgiving sales contest was announced during my second week in the field, I figured it had been created just for me. I committed myself to victory.

Now I rose at six in the morning, instead of seven, so I could arrive at the far end of my territory when the first grocer opened. Instead of 10 store visits a day, I squeezed in 15. On Saturdays and Sundays I was in Stop & Shop stores building displays of Tide and Joy under red and orange displays featuring turkeys, pumpkins, and pilgrims. When my brother from Ohio came out for a visit, he helped haul cases of detergent from back rooms to assemble displays.

My objective was clear: to win the contest on my way to the top of the company. That inspired my goals each day: more dealer ads, more sales, and more boxes of detergent stacked in turkey displays. I was active, active, active, firing lots of arrows, many of which missed the target altogether and few of which hit the center.

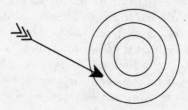

However, when the contest ended, just before Thanksgiving, and the results were tabulated, it turned out that enough of my arrows had scored to achieve the objective I set. Two weeks later, I stood before all 30 salespeople in the New England region. "Congratulations," said the sales manager, handing me a check for $25. "You will now be known, forever more, as TOP TUR-KEY."

(The next month, back in Cincinnati at P & G headquarters, I was no longer top turkey. I was turkey enough, though, to make a few mistakes and get mediocre job reviews. Less than two years later I was gone, off to San Francisco and a new life.)

If you want to be top turkey, or tops in anything, focus on your purpose in life and on the mission needed to achieve it. Figure out what it takes to get there, the big steps and the little ones. Be willing to change both yourself and your target. Focus on objectives, not obstacles. As they say at IBM, "Obstacles are what we see when we take our eyes off the goal."

The obstacles you see may be pink slips or a downturn in the economy. You may face rejection, competition, or catastrophe. You will survive it all if you stay true to your developing sense of mission, to the unfolding of your life purpose. As Nietzsche said, "That which does not kill me makes me stronger."

Success Strategy: See obstacles as opportunities. Look beyond difficulties to the changes and knowledge you will surely find on the other side. Face tough times with one eye on happy outcomes.

Human beings are purposeful by nature, according to philosophers. We are teleological, to use a scientific term meaning there is purpose in both human and natural processes. *Teleos* is a Greek word for "complete," and this is what we seek—completeness. Each of us is drawn toward completion at the end of a day, or a year, or a lifetime.

I encourage you to respect your own personal teleology, to notice what it is that you are inspired to complete today, this year, this lifetime.

Take Rob. He wants to be the top sales executive in the manufacturing company where he has worked for two years. So he asked for a written assessment by his supervisors and the heads of credit and production. "Temper is a big problem," said one. "Abusive, demeaning, unprofessional," said another. Several said, "Rob is not a team player." There were plenty of positive comments, too, about market knowledge and customer awareness. But even these called Rob "difficult" and "arrogant."

How has Rob reacted? He sees these comments as a big help in achieving his objective. He has changed in response to these reactions, become more considerate and more willing to help others. He has just finished his best sales year ever, with an income well into six figures, and he is closer than ever to being number one at his company—and perhaps even a VP.

Rob stays focused on his objectives, no matter what obstacles he encounters. How about you?

EXPLORATION: What Keeps Me from Getting What I Want? What obstacles do I face in my work? Which have I created for myself? Which have I made more formidable than necessary? Which are beyond my control? Write these down and note at least one thing you can do to overcome each obstacle.

CHAPTER
21

Go for the Best, Go for It Often

If happiness is activity in accordance with
excellence, it is reasonable that it should
be in accordance with the highest
excellence.

—Aristotle

Take your work seriously, not yourself.

—Dwight David Eisenhower

Do the best job of which you are capable,
then reach for a point even beyond that.

—Alfred Stieglitz

"She looked right past me as if I were transparent," Juan Hamilton recalls of his first meeting with Georgia O'Keeffe. Hamilton had gone to her home with a friend and "was overwhelmed" upon meeting the 84-year-old superstar of American art. She ignored him. Undeterred, the 26-year-old potter went again to the artist's home, this time to help unload a Franklin stove. Again, O'Keeffe ignored him. Virginia Kirby, a local writer who worked for O'Keeffe, suggested a different approach. "Just go on your own," she told Hamilton. "Don't try to get anyone to introduce you."

So early one morning Hamilton knocked on the artist's back door and said that he was interested in work. The housekeeper relayed the message to O'Keeffe, who was in her studio, and when she came to the door her response was "Work? I don't have any work."

Hamilton turned to leave.

"Wait a minute," called O'Keeffe. "Can you pack a shipping crate?" Hamilton said he could.

As they worked the next day O'Keeffe said, "You speak pretty good English. Did you finish high school?" When she learned that Hamilton had completed college and two semesters of graduate school, she asked, "Can you type?"

Hamilton could, and although it took several months before O'Keeffe remembered his name, Hamilton's perseverance led to a close friendship during the remaining years of the painter's life, a friendship in which they learned about one another's art and traveled together to many parts of the world.

When O'Keeffe's death, just two years shy of her one-hundredth birthday, ended their 13-year friendship, Hamilton was left with some wonderful memories and responsibility for much of her valuable art. He still refers to her as Miss O'Keeffe, with obvious respect and affection. "Her work," he writes, "is a mirror of the person we have lost."

Hamilton aimed for the best—for a chance to know one of the world's great artists. And he persevered—returning even when O'Keeffe did not remember his name. Hamilton found the balance point between his goal and rejection, between quality and persistence.

Go for the Best

What's best for you or for me may not be what is the best for Juan Hamilton. What we can learn from his relationship with Georgia O'Keeffe is the value of having a vision and sense of purpose whether one is an artist or a teacher or salesperson. We see the importance of knocking at the door of opportunity again, and again, and again.

How do you know what's best for you? In relationships it doesn't have to be a genius like Georgia O'Keeffe, but it should be someone further along the path, someone with something to teach you. In achievement it doesn't have to be the highest, but it should be something that brings out the best in you, tapping into untested inner resources. Like the track star, go for a personal record—aim for what you've never done before. Given a choice between the best and second best, set your sights on the higher star.

Success Strategy: Aim high, a little beyond where you think you can reach. Use your goals to keep growing and getting better. Test yourself. Stretch.

How do you know what's high enough for you? Think back to the archer's target mentioned earlier. What is your purpose? What is your mission? What are the major goals in your life today? With all those in sight, you will have a clearer vision of what "the best" is for you.

How do you "go for the best"? This book is full of suggestions and one way to pull them all together is to make a plan. Like Julius Caesar leading an army or Imelda Marcos on a shopping spree, we need a vision of what lies ahead, a conception of what we want the future to be. In making a plan for your life or your business or your next shopping trip, there are five basic questions—simple in structure, often difficult to answer well.

1. **Where am I starting from?** What shape am I in—physically, emotionally, financially—overall? Self-assessment is the starting point of all effective plans and this involves a look backward. What have I learned about myself and the world in the experiences that brought me to where I am today?
2. **What resources do I have?** In work-life planning, the most important resources to consider are the talent, knowledge, and passion we have for meeting challenges in our daily lives. The second most important resources are human: family, friends, contacts who will support us in our quest for the best. After these are resources such as time and money.
3. **Where am I going?** For most of us, this is the toughie. The

answer comes from pondering our purpose in life, our mission and objectives, what is "the best" for us. Even those who say, "I don't know" usually have some intuitive sense for a life direction. Our challenge is to keep asking, to keep improving on the answer, to sharpen our focus. Each day we move forward with an imperfect vision of the future, in the knowledge that the picture will get clearer, next month and next year.

4. **How will I get there?** Today more than ever, there are many options in our lives. An effective plan contains thoughtfully considered alternatives for arriving at the goal: Plan A and Plan B and maybe even Plan C. You may decide to conduct exploratory interviews at the half-dozen top companies in the field of your choice; an alternative might be to take a temporary job on the path to the work of your dreams. This part of planning usually allows for adjustments as feedback comes in from the outside world, which helps us become more flexible and responsive to new information.

5. **How will I start?** In business this is called operational planning. What am I going to do tomorrow and next week? What are my goals for achieving the objectives that will accomplish my mission? In work-life planning this is: Who will I call and where will I go to do research and what will I put in writing by when? The "by when" is important because all plans need target dates and achievement mileposts to accompany purpose and vision.

If you are not quite sure how to create a plan for your life, don't despair: there are as many ways to plan as there are people. Some do it all in their heads and some do it on the backs of envelopes. Some think ahead 10 years, whereas other very successful people rarely think ahead more than a few weeks. Some do right-brain planning with pictures, others do left-brain planning with written words, and still others do both, blending creativity with logic. Some get outside input and others plan by themselves. However you do it, I encourage you to become more skillful in harnessing the power of planning, to find new ways to make your life better, to bring more of the best into your world.

A real estate entrepreneur I admire has a "focus room" near

his office, where he and his senior executives review strategies on the many projects they manage. "We think about the future in there, about opportunities and potential disasters," he says, "what we'll do if there's an earthquake or building moratorium." The walls are covered with maps, charts, and an idea board for pinning notes on "property management," "new projects," and "ways to add quality."

If you had a focus room, where would it be? If you had a wall for planning your life, what would you have up there? If you found time for something like this, what would you focus on?

After the Final No

"After the final no," writes Wallace Stevens, "comes a yes. And on that yes, all the world depends." Nothing important was ever accomplished without rejection, and usually lots of it. No plan works without perseverance. Consider these examples, all based on real people and real successes:

- A young man seeks a job with IBM, even though he knows they only hire college graduates, which he is not, and refuses to give up despite dozens of rejections. He reads everything he can find about IBM and the computer industry. He talks with IBM salespeople and customers and competitors. He visits the IBM office 16 times over a 14-month period. He gets the job—and becomes a superstar.
- A Beatles fan wants to meet John Lennon so much that she not only writes letters to him and phones him, but she creates a plan to jump into Lennon's limousine to meet her idol. Not only did she get the seat beside Lennon, displacing his then-wife, but eventually Yoko Ono becomes Mrs. Lennon.
- A teacher who wants to give students a summer learning experience in Europe writes dozens of letters to colleges there, most of which go unanswered. He calls friends, talks to students, and lets the world know his dream. One who hears the dream has just come back from the Sorbonne in Paris,

where the dream finally became reality, two years after the first rejection.

If there is a final no between you and your dream, why not arrive at that final no sooner rather than later? Why not start now to hear every no that comes before it? Why not get the inevitable rejections behind you—without being impetuous about it—and get to the yes at the end of the rainbow?

"Luck loves the active," says the sixth law. "Luck favors bodies in motion." More good things happen to those in circulation than to those fixed in space or time. The more active you are, the more likely you are to get what you want. So make that extra phone call, write that extra note, take the extra moment to tell an acquaintance about your work dream. Aim high. Fire often. The last effort may be the one that pays off.

Success Strategy: Celebrate near misses. When you go for the best, getting close is also plenty good. Honor that. Congratulate yourself and the others involved.

Two Dozen Donuts

A sales executive in the financial printing industry had been pursuing a major client for three years. He had called, he had written, he had flown in from San Francisco to take the buyer and the buyer's boss to lunch. All to no avail.

His perseverance led to the discovery that this client had a major printing project for a new stock offering coming up. Within hours, the executive got an okay to submit a proposal for the job. "We really wanted this business," he told me later. "We were hungry and we were ready."

The crucial buying decision was to be made at 9 A.M. Thursday in the client's Salt Lake City headquarters. The other bidder on the job, a major corporation in Dallas, submitted their proposal by fax. The sales executive from San Francisco, however, flew in the night before with the proposal in his briefcase. At 7 A.M. on Thursday, he went to the best bakery in town—he had done his research—picked up two dozen donuts, and drove to the offices of his prospective client, where he waited in the snow on the front steps. When the Chief Financial Officer of the corporation arrived a half hour later, he was astounded.

"How did you know that's my favorite bakery?" He laughed. "How did you know I love donuts?"

The two men spent 15 minutes together, joking about the donuts and discussing details of the proposal. Then the CFO went into his meeting, while the sales executive from San Francisco caught the mid-morning flight home. It took several days more and a number of phone calls for the salesman from San Francisco to get to the final yes, but the real decision had been made on that snowy Thursday morning.

In your search for work that is right for you, why not be as bold as the printing salesman? Instead of a proposal you may present a cover letter and a customized résumé. Instead of donuts you might show up with apples. Whatever you do, why not show that you care enough to be there in person? Why not be the candidate to make the extra effort? Why not be the one to hear the yes on which all the world depends?

EXPLORATION: Where Can I Raise My Sights? How can I focus more clearly on my personal dream? What can I do to become more active in making it come true? What do I need to do to become the one to hear the yes on which all the world depends?

CHAPTER

22

Talk Straight

Truthful words are not beautiful;
  beautiful words are not truthful.
Good words are not persuasive;
  persuasive words are not good.

—Lao-tzu

The greater your dreams, the more terrible
your nightmares.

—Edward Abbey

Honest tea is the best policy.

—Herb Caen

Long, long ago in a country beyond the sea that is beyond the sea, high up on a mountainside in an ancient castle, lived a king and a queen and all their court, the most famous of whom were the chef, who was known for his creativity, and the jester, who was known for his wisdom.

One evening at dinner in the great hall, after the plates from the third course had been cleared, the doors leading to the kitchen swung open and two heralds replendent in gold and crimson trumpeted in the chef, all in white except for the cordon bleu over his breast. On his outstretched hands rested a blue velvet pillow and on the pillow was a golden serving plate; on the plate, steaming hot and shimmering in the candlelight, was a food that no one in the kingdom had ever before seen.

As the chef approached the high table, the whole hall was

filled with a pungent aroma, heightened by butter and spices and Marsala wine. No one had ever smelled anything so delicious before.

When the chef placed the golden platter before the king, his eyes sparkled with anticipation. As the silent hall waited, the king took the golden fork handed to him by the chef and after inhaling deeply, lifted a single bite to his mouth.

"This is wonderful," exclaimed the king. "Pray tell, chef, what is it?"

"This, sire, is a vegetable," replied the chef, "called cauliflower."

"Truly," said the jester, "cauliflower is the most wonderful vegetable in the whole world."

"Henceforth," said the king, "cauliflower shall be served at every meal, in the morning, at midday, in the evening—whenever my subjects gather to eat in this kingdom. So it is proclaimed."

If you have ever eaten cauliflower, and if you use your imagination, you can guess what happened. It was on the sixth day, in the great hall, when the plate heaped with cauliflower was presented to the king. First he rolled his eyes heavenward and then he put his hand over his mouth. "Ahhhhrrrr."

Then he slammed down his fork and said, "I hate this, I DETEST it. Cauliflower is awful!"

"Truly," said the jester, "cauliflower is the most awful vegetable in the whole world."

"Wait a minute," said the king to the jester, after thinking for a moment. "Less than a week ago you said that cauliflower was the most wonderful vegetable in the whole world and now you say it is the most awful. Pray tell, fool, how can this be?"

"The answer to your question, sire, is a simple one." The jester smiled. "It is because I serve the king and not the cauliflower."

After telling this story in a workshop, the next thing I do is invite participants to ponder where their service is dedicated. I ask them, as I ask you: Does your loyalty lie with the vegetable of the day, or with the king?

> **Success Strategy:** Reconsider your loyalties. How have your priorities shifted over time? What is at the top of the list today? What else ranks up there? Think big.

Straight Talk

In olden days straight talk could mean losing one's head, especially if it reached a vindictive king, but nowadays it almost always produces a felicitous result—sooner or later, one way or another. Dick is manager of a branch office for a medium-size bank and when he complained for the third time to his boss, a senior VP, about poor communication, the boss exploded. "What the hell do you mean, poor communication? You get dozens of memos and bulletins and faxes every week!"

Dick gulped. "No one told us about the MasterCard promotion that came out in Tuesday's paper." He paused. "And when customers started asking about it, the tellers and platform people felt foolish."

That communicated. "I'm glad you told me," said the senior VP. "Now you're talking. I'm glad to have it straight."

Straight talk means different things to each of us, whether we're managing a branch office or looking for the right work. But there are common principles for effective, authentic communication, including these:

- **Think first.** Before opening your mouth, be sure what you want to accomplish. Taste your words before you spit them out. Examine your motivation. Be sure you know where you are coming from.
- **Get permission.** Not everyone wants to hear straight talk. It's better if the person to whom it is directed has given or implied permission for candor. On the other hand, it's easier to ask forgiveness than to ask permission.
- **Find the right time and place.** Not only should you find the

right person with whom to communicate, you should do it where you will not be overheard and where you will not be interrupted.

- **Beware of group think.** When the decision was being made to launch the Bay of Pigs invasion of Cuba, President Kennedy's closest advisers were influenced by the military. Voices of caution were drowned out and the result was disastrous. The message? Think for yourself, talk for yourself. Group think does not produce the best results.

- **Focus on issues, not personalities.** Talk straight about assignments, money, results. Avoid blaming and judging. As a friend once commented, "You can have their ass if you leave them their face." Do not demean, do not diminish anyone's dignity, and remember, bosses have feelings too.

- **Aspire to brevity.** Keep it short. Be like the Yale University applicant who in response to the instruction, "In one page or less, describe your greatest strength," wrote a single word: "succinctness." (She got in.)

- **Aspire to simplicity.** When given the choice between a simple, common word and one of many syllables, choose simplicity. One of the great masters of our language, Winston Churchill, said, "Short words are best and old words when short are best of all."

- **Aspire to honesty.** Aim to be honest. Tell the truth, even though that may seem unusual in an era of lies about Santa Claus, fatal diseases, company profits, covert military activities, and the mileage your best friend gets on his car.

- **Feelings never lie.** When in doubt, check your gut. Most of us have an extraordinary capacity for rationalization and self-deception. The mind can deceive, feelings do not. If you feel anxious or fearful or angry, some aspect of the truth is being hidden. Discover what it is before speaking and consider including it in what you say. Straight talk often begins with disclosing feelings.

- **Speak for yourself.** When you focus on feelings, it is best to speak for yourself. When you talk about your passion, for instance, you are more effective than when you talk about someone else. Implied judgments, made by you or by "they" or "them," are not straight talk and usually alienate your listener.

- **Ask for a second chance.** When you get it wrong, say, "Sorry, I blew it," and try again. Most people will forgive if presented with a candid apology and good intent. Even if they don't, what have you lost?
- **Avoid dullness.** "Of all the sins," Frank Capra liked to say, "the cardinal sin is dullness." Do not bore people. Speak with authenticity and emotion. When you reveal feelings, you hold the attention of your listeners.
- **Keep learning.** Read at least one newspaper daily and one newsmagazine weekly. Watch educational TV shows and videos. Listen to informative radio programs and tapes. Attend courses, lectures, workshops, and seminars. Learn as though you were going to live forever.

Talking straight is not easy. It is as hard when you're talking about work as it is when you're talking above love, and that is plenty hard. It is hard because our self-esteem and our passion and our livelihood are involved. No matter how difficult it is, and no matter how often you fall short of the mark, aim to talk straight. More fulfilling work and more satisfying work relationships are the payoff.

Success Strategy: When in doubt, return to purpose. Ask yourself how your words match your mission in life. If you are moved by ego or anger, remember that your ultimate service is to something larger than yourself.

Talk Smart

It's Saturday morning during a weekend workshop and participants are focused on barriers between them and what they want in their lives, on what keeps them from reaching their goals. There are 25 people in the room and several have already confronted their barriers, working one at a time with a facilitator. It's not yet noon and already there have been tears and anger, shouts and laughter.

"I'd like a turn," says an agitated young woman, who turns out to be a 29-year-old IBM sales executive.

"What's the issue?"

"It's my boss, Rhonda" she says. "I hate that woman."

"Imagine this pillow is Rhonda and tell her how you feel, okay?"

"I hate you, Rhonda; I really do."

"Tell her."

"I hate you with every molecule in my body!"

"Yes?"

"I wish you every kind of ill that could possibly befall you!"

"Tell her."

"Rhonda, I'd like to seduce your husband."

After some uneasy laughter around the room, she continued, "I'd like to seduce him so well that all the rest of his life he'd never forget the experience."

When the laughter subsides and the passion fades, it becomes clear to everyone that the real issue is not Rhonda, not the boss, but the employer and the work style. The real issue is not at all what it seemed in the beginning.

"I need to leave IBM," the young woman concludes. "Rhonda and I can be friends, actually, once I get my act together and find work I really care about in an environment where I can get the respect I want."

By the end of the weekend, she has a plan for developing other career options and eventually making Rhonda part of her plans. She has explored her feelings and their origin. She knows more about the barriers before her and is ready to surmount them. Her emotional experience has prepared her for the straight talk that will lead her toward the life she yearns for. Her candor has prepared her to talk smart.

EXPLORATION: To Whom Do I Need to Talk Straight? List five people with whom you would like to be more honest. What would you like to say to each? How do you plan to proceed?

In work and in life, there is great value to be found in straight talk. In work and in life, the more we practice the better we get. So start today to be more candid, more expressive, more authentic. Don't delay. Put your money on honest tea.

CHAPTER

23

Work Smart

Whatsoever thy hand findest to do, do
with all thy might.

—Ecclesiastes 9:10

Now I get me up to work,
I pray the Lord I will not shirk;
If I should die before the night,
I pray the Lord my work's all right.

—Jack London

The quickest thinking is the thinking of
the body, and the body thinks surely,
effortlessly, because it is not soaked in
character, as the brain is.

—E. L. Doctorow, *Billy Bathgate*

"Three days a week. For twenty years that is all I have worked,
though I have not been a couch potato. Far from it. In those two
decades I wrote fourteen books, taught dozens of classes, con-
sulted with hundreds of clients, and gave hundreds of talks to
thousands of people. In each of those years I skied at least forty
days and ran at least one river."

This unusual man, talented and full of energy, is Jay Conrad
Levinson, and he is the first to say that his unorthodox work style
is not appropriate for everyone. Some people can't limit their
work week to Monday, Tuesday, and Wednesday, as Jay does.
Some people don't want to spend all day Thursday with friends,

as Jay does, or all day Saturday with a spouse. Some people don't want to work as hard as Jay does, even for three days a week.

Work Hard

Most of us know all about hard, boring, demeaning work. Most of us have had ill-fitting, uninspiring, unpleasant jobs that we came to hate. To work hard at something we love is different. That kind of work is hard but fun. It is more fun if we do it well, using ideas like these:

• **Use time skillfully.** The most important gift we have is time. Like any gift, it should be appreciated, cherished, respected. The time in your life dedicated to your work should be 100 percent time, where all your energy and all your attention are devoted to whatever it is you are working on. To learn how Jay Levinson does it, read his book *The Ninety Minute Hour.*

• **Do it right the first time.** When your total focus is on the work before you, it is not hard to make decisions about letters, phone calls, and human interactions. In all you do, in big things and little things, aspire to excellence. As you go through the day keep asking: Am I doing the right work? To paraphrase Peter Drucker, "Efficiency is doing the work right. Effectiveness is doing the right work." Aim to be *both* efficient *and* effective.

• **Stay on track.** Watch for distractions. Be willing to follow your instincts down unplanned paths over the course of a workday, but make sure you see how such side trips lead to your ultimate destination. Be ruthless in pursuit of your purpose. Keep your eye on the items at the top of your TO DO list. Remember the words of Jay Levinson, who says, "As you learn about time, you begin to learn how little it is related to clocks and how much it is related to priorities."

• **Let others know you are working hard.** If you telephone Jay Levinson on a Tuesday afternoon, you know instantly that he is working. He may talk for 30 seconds or he may agree to call you back, but he is absolutely unabashed about letting others know he is working. Be like Jay and let the good word get out that when you are working, you are working hard.

- **Encourage others to work hard, too.** Sooner or later, they will thank you for it.

Julie Greenwalt, Detroit bureau chief for *People* magazine, is a self-described workaholic. "You don't have time to see friends, or just go to the movies" when working 60-hour weeks, she says. She is not happy and not even sure she's being effective. "Why do I do it? That's a good question. Working like this is an addiction. You feel guilty if you work only eight hours a day."

Working hard does not mean working all the time. It does not mean feeling guilty when you are not working. In fact, one of the main reasons for working hard is to have balance in your life, so you can feel good about work—and also play and love and all the other nonwork activities that add meaning to your life. It is so you will have significant chunks of time to be with friends or family, to take classes or play tennis or visit the art museum.

"I'm a leisuraholic," Dick Bolles once said with a smile. "I believe in fun along with work." When I later described this addiction to a class, one of the students spoke up. "I can do Bolles one better," said Kent Massey. "I'm a frolicaholic." Be like Bolles and Massey: Live fully, passionately, purposefully—but balance your work with leisure and frolic.

Success Strategy: Make time technology your servant, not your master. Use car phones, pagers, fax machines, and other technology to enhance your life, not diminish it. Make it work for you, not vice versa.

Draw, Antonio!

After the Italian master Michelangelo died, the story is told, his apprentice went to the studio and found a note, handwritten by the 89-year-old master. It read, "Draw, Antonio, draw, Antonio, draw, and do not waste time!"

When you are on a roll, keep rolling. Do not waste time.

When you are hot, keep the streak going. You do not need to work for dozens of hours or hundreds of days. You will know when your productive period is over. When you are going, give it all you have. Work with passion, but don't overdo it.

Vector In

Sir Isaac Newton wrote *Philosophiae Naturalis Principia Mathematica* in 1687, at the urging of friends to whom we owe a great debt, for without their encouragement we would not have the Second Law of Motion, which applies equally to the physical world and the world of work.

Newton's Second Law tells what happens when force is applied to a moving body using the formula $F = ma$, where F is force, m is mass moved, and a is acceleration. This law describes the importance of vectors—forces of differing magnitudes acting in differing directions—in moving mass. In lay terms, this means that more is achieved when forces acting on a single point all work in the same direction. It's like horses pulling apart or pulling together:

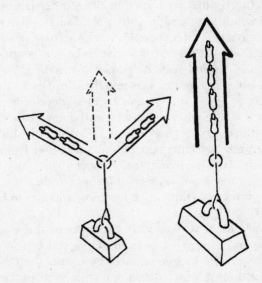

If we aspire to be effective, we want all our horses pulling in the same direction. We don't want one inner voice shouting, "This way!" while another cries, "No! the other way!" We want all our horses to see the same vision and pull for it. We want our head and our heart, our thoughts and our dreams, our inner voices and our energy all to be in harmony.

Work Smart

Working smart means applying some basic principles, many of which you already know about if you have read this far:

• **Plan.** Begin your work with the right tools, the right supplies, and the right allies—always remembering your purpose and mission, your goals and objectives. Plan for changes in plan, so you have extra resources, including time. Learn what your best planning style is. Follow it and develop it and make that style your own, no matter what you read in books like this.

• **Get help.** Work is a social process—we may do much of it by ourselves, but eventually all work involves other people. Become skillful at including others in your work life as advisers, helpers, colleagues, coaches, idea people, and compassionate listeners. Remember the most powerful sentence in the language: I have a problem and I need your help. Use it often.

• **Be flexible.** No matter how much you plan and how much help you have, there will be unexpected developments. There will be points where you are blocked and a new path is better. Be resilient at those points. Stay relaxed. Practice flexibility.

• **Listen well.** Working smart means learning from others. It means integrating feedback and new information from many sources. It means interpreting subtle and indirect messages. If you want to work smart, practice listening and aim to become excellent at it.

• **Look ahead.** Give your full attention to the work you are doing today and tomorrow, but remember to keep your head up and one eye on the bigger picture. Dive into the drama of the moment but do not let it distract you from your purpose. Let every act contribute in some way, large or small, to your mission. Focus. Vector in.

As you traverse the cycles in your work life, you will learn more about what working smart means for you. You will get ideas from this book and from a hundred other sources. You will try approaches that do not work or do not last. Some ideas will be just right for you, though, and out of this will come your own individual style.

EXPLORATION: How Can I Work Smarter? Make a list of five ways you can be more effective in your work. Beside each item on your list write what you will do about it and by when.

The summer I was 17, I got a job on a cattle ranch in Wolf Creek, Montana. It was a working ranch, running cattle and sheep, but I spent more time stacking alfalfa hay than working livestock. There were usually five or six in the bunkhouse, and we were out before dawn for pancakes and bacon and a truck ride to the field for 12 hours of gritty labor.

The pay was $100 a month or a penny for each bale stacked, plus room and board, and poker lessons never exceeded $2 a night. Fred Potts, Earl Tubbs, and I worked as a team and the month we stacked 110,000 bales my check was $110. The Montana skies were glorious, the work was healthy, and I cherish vivid memories of the colorful characters I came to know that summer.

I worked hard, for sure, and maybe even smart. The foreman called me a good hand, which meant a lot at the time, and I outgrew my boyhood dream of becoming a cattle rancher, though I also learned that I love the independent life of the cowboy. Did then, still do.

That summer of 1954 was full of discoveries for me and the best, the one that remains with me, is that there is nothing wrong with hard work as long as we're wise enough to learn from it.

CHAPTER

24

Mentor Magic

I'm just a plowhand from Arkansas, but I
have learned how to hold a team together.
You have to lift some up, and calm others
down, until finally they've got one
heartbeat together. That's all it takes to get
people to win.

—Coach "Bear" Bryant

In the multitude of counselors there is
safety.

—Proverbs 11:14

A mentor is a person who *oversees* the
career and development of another
person, usually a junior, through teaching,
counseling, and providing psychological
support, protecting, and at times
promoting or sponsoring.

—Michael Zey, *The Mentor Connection*

"I am myself obtaining for you the fast ship," says Mentor to the
son of Odysseus in the Homeric epic poem. "I shall be of your
company aboard her." Telemachus has grown to manhood under
the watchful eye of Mentor, the comrade to whom his traveling
father had committed his house, "enjoining all in it to be obedi-
ent to the old man and in his steadfast guard."
Have you ever felt that you could use a fast ship in the jour-

ney toward your purpose? Might you like an ally on board? Ever think how your life would be different if you had someone like the original Mentor to support you in the adventure?

The mythical Mentor is male but not always, not really. Sometimes he is something more: the embodiment of Athena, daughter of Zeus, who appears "like Mentor in form and voice" to offer aid to those on heroic missions. Among the gods and goddesses on Mount Olympus, Athena is second only to her father in power and position.

Known for her creativity, inventiveness, and persuasiveness, Athena represents justice, mercy, and wisdom as she influences heroic lives in the *Odyssey* "talking and looking like Mentor." Mentor is male in form, but Greek mythology invites us to see a larger figure, one integrating the strong feminine energy of a great goddess. It is only natural that your mentors, in this time and in our culture, can be both male and female.

Finding Mentors

For Odysseus, finding Mentor was not hard: he was a member of the royal household. While you may find a mentor in your own family, you will also have to look beyond. What you're looking for, essentially, is three kinds of support:

• **Coaching,** which is specific advice for short-term action. A coach helps you answer the question: what should I do next and how should I do it? Coaching is helpful in preparing for a sporting event, an examination, a job interview, or a business meeting. You want someone like "Bear" Bryant to lift you up or calm you down. You want someone to give you suggestions and demonstrations about how to do it right. If it is skillful coaching, it will help you perform well as long as you live. **To find coaching,** look for experts with specific experience doing whatever it is you want to learn how to do. If you want to get better at acting, find a drama coach. If you want to make better presentations, find a speech coach—a friend of mine, for instance, used Lee Glickstein (a speaking and humor coach in San Francisco) to help prepare his acceptance speech when he was being honored for donating $100,000 to a nearby community center. Although some coaching relationships are long-lasting, most are not. You do not need to like this person, but he or she should be someone you respect and can work comfortably with short term.

• **Counseling** is interactive advice for short- and midterm action. Counselors listen as well as talk, integrating your knowledge and experience with their advice. Counseling is important for larger and more complex issues than those that call for coaching. Skillful counselors bring out the best in you while teaching you new approaches to problem solving. **To find counseling,** look for experts who have already been through the kind of experience you are facing. If you are looking for a job, find a career counselor. If you are dealing with alcohol addiction, find a substance-abuse expert. A counselor should be someone you respect and trust enough to be candid with, like my friend George who advises people who run small businesses. It should be someone you are willing to work with long-term. You may have more than one counselor, in different parts of your life, but it is unlikely that you will have a multitude. First listen to others, then listen to your own heart.

• **Mentoring** is guidance, inspiration, and support over the long pull. It may be a 20-year relationship, like the original Mentor had with the son of Odysseus, or it may be longer. It will probably involve coaching and counseling but also something more: compassion and a caring commitment. Some people, if you asked, would tell you they never had a mentor, and others think in terms of just one, which is okay, but the more expansive view is that mentoring is available in many forms from more than one person in many parts of your life. No single individual has it all to give you, so it is wise to accept mentoring gifts wherever you find them. **To find mentoring** look among your coaches and counselors, first, and then among others with the capacity to enlarge your life. Mentoring can be had from parents, teachers, bosses, and professional colleagues. Unlike coaching or counseling, you cannot find mentoring in the Yellow Pages. Jay Levinson, the author described in the previous chapter, has been a wonderful mentor to me; I met him in a workshop given by his literary agent. Some mentors actively seek out protégés, and you might be found in this way, but usually you need to do the initiating: ask for some time, ask for a meeting (I asked Jay to lunch), ask for advice. Then keep asking and keep listening. Look for re-lationships that can mature into something special. See it as three circles, each larger than the other:

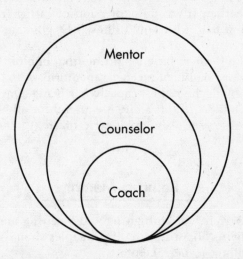

Mentoring can happen in many ways: by example, for in-stance, or by advice and support given verbally or in writing or through others. It can happen in a relationship that is intimate and revealing, or in one more distant and aloof; with someone older, which is most typical, or, in some rewarding exceptions, with someone younger than you. It can be direct and with your knowledge, which is most typical, or indirect—where you have been blessed and are only aware of it later.

> **Success Strategy:** Seek exemplars. When you are about to leave town, leave a career, or leave your spouse, look to some-one who successfully completed a similar life change. Learn all you can about how they succeeded.

Gregory Bateson, the anthropologist, was an intellectual men-tor of mine. One Saturday morning in April of 1980 during a workshop on movement and poetry near Big Sur, he gave me a big hug. He was six feet six, my height, and the hug brought tears pouring down my face.

"Are you okay?" Gregory asked. I could only nod in gratitude, for it was the hug I never received from my father, who had died six months earlier. It was an expression of caring from another man I loved, a man who would himself be gone, at age 76, just 90 days later.

Gregory and others have taught me that one of the best ways to become more skillful at receiving mentoring is to learn how to mentor. Although the richest capacity for being a mentor usually starts in the middle of one's life, it is useful for all of us, regardless of where we are in the great cycle of life, to know how it is done.

Being a Mentor

In my experience of both giving and receiving mentoring and talking to clients about it, several principles should be followed if you are willing to be a mentor:

- **Say Yes.** Look for opportunities to respond positively. Few of us go through a day without saying no to a number of things, but each of us can look for opportunities to give back some of the teaching and love we have received along the way. Be like an entrepreneur I know, a highly successful woman, who says, "I always say yes until I understand the question."
- **Make Time.** Save some of your most precious commodity for unexpected opportunities to be with someone who needs your help. General Georges Doriot at the Harvard Business School taught his students to "be tough and smart in scheduling your life, but leave some flexibility so you can follow your instincts and give time to someone who doesn't expect it." Say yes, sometimes, to the persistent, but also remember those who are less demanding.
- **Initiate.** No matter how busy you are, reach out to someone who might benefit from what you have learned, from the

power you have accumulated, from the experiences in your life. Reward yourself with the satisfaction that comes from making use of what life has taught you.

- **Just Do It.** Go ahead without wondering where this will lead or if it is coaching, counseling, mentoring, or something that cannot be labeled. Be honest and fair, but don't worry about what it is called. Like the athlete in the ad, just do it.

- **Trust Your Instincts.** Be candid and expressive as a mentor. Listen to your feelings; honor your experience. If intuition tells you something out of the ordinary, speak up, even if it makes you uncomfortable. It's fine to be like Winston Churchill, who loved learning but hated to sit in the classroom. Focus on the ready-to-learn part of those you serve and your service will have value.

- **Discourage Exploitation.** When your instincts tell you someone is exploiting your willingness to be a mentor, try the results test. Do the results suggest that real listening is going on? Do the results suggest that your efforts are adding value? If not, and if you still sense that you are being used for selfish purposes, back away from the relationship.

- **Cultivate Loyalty** in yourself and those you serve. Develop patience for personal foibles and the little ups and downs of life, in yourself and others. Practice tolerance. Be willing to play the game, full tilt, all the way to the final whistle. Expect the same from others.

EXPLORATION: Who Are My Mentors? Make a list of the coaches, counselors, and mentors in your life. Include everyone you can think of, even if you are not sure where they fit in. Put a star beside the names of those most important to you. Express gratitude to someone on your list.

Blessing

Back in Chapter 19, "Do What You Love, Love What You Do," the young woman in the Grimms' fairy tale was taken in as an orphaned child by a godmother who "educated her in all that was good." When the girl was 15, her godmother, by now an old woman, said, "Dear daughter, I feel my end drawing near" and laid her hands on the girl's head, blessing her. "The blessing of the good old woman was on all that she did," the story says, on the flax that increased of its own accord, on the carpet she wove more beautiful than the eyes of man had ever yet beheld, on her royal wedding. We all need blessings like this in our own lives if we are to find wholeness and happiness.

My life has been blessed by Robert Bly, a poet-minstrel-teacher 10 years my senior. Bly has taught me about fathers and sons and poetry. He has challenged me, confronted me, and awakened me—with bouzouki music and song as I lay in a sleeping bag one cold dawn in the Mendocino woods. I have learned from Bly about blessings, and through Bly from one of his teachers, the Irish poet William Butler Yeats.

"Yeats was a mentor to me," Bly said in San Antonio not long ago, "even though I never met him. Can you see how that could be?" Bly knows about mentoring and he loves to recite some lines from Yeats, which suggest that the Irishman knew about it too:

> My fiftieth year had come and gone,
> I sat, a solitary man,
> In a crowded London shop,
> An open book and empty cup
> Upon a marble table top.
>
> While on the shop and street I gazed
> My body of a sudden blazed;
> And twenty minutes more or less
> It seemed so great my happiness,
> That I was blessèd and could bless.

25

Failing to Succeed

Failure is impossible.

—Susan B. Anthony, on her
eighty-sixth birthday

There is the greatest practical benefit to
making a few failures early in life.

—Thomas Huxley, 1870

Failure is not about our unworthiness or
powerlessness. Failure is an opportunity
for learning—about inaccurate pictures of
current reality, about strategies that didn't
work as expected, about the clarity of the
vision.

—Peter Senge

"You may condemn the man who tried to force the Dardanelles,"
Winston Churchill told Parliament, "but your children will keep
their condemnation for those who did not rally to their aid." It
was 1915 and the architect of a bold plan to end World War I was
forced to resign as First Lord of the Admiralty when his plan
failed. Churchill, age 41, was without political office for the first
time in 10 years.

"He had the best strategic sense in the government," said *The
Manchester Guardian*, but it made no difference. Churchill had
failed. It did not matter that the battle was lost to the attacking
forces by "those who did not rally to their aid." It was to be a

quarter of a century before Churchill was fully vindicated as the brilliant strategist who saved England in World War II. Out of one of the great failures of the twentieth century came one of the most astounding successes.

Nobody comes to an authentic sense of purpose—in war or in peace—without failures. Nobody achieves meaningful success without making mistakes and paying dearly. The challenge we all face is to try, again and again, even when we fail.

Trying and Failing

"It's tough trying to crack the job market as a 48-year-old woman," says Melissa, an attractive, energetic writer and trainer. "It's been over a year now and all the rejection is wearing me down. I've mailed hundreds of résumés and had dozens of interviews. I'm damn good at this game."

The pain is palpable as Melissa, impeccably attired, describes her frustration.

"There was a corporate communications job at Levi Strauss that I'd be perfect for. My skills and experience matched the job description to a T, and the chemistry with my prospective boss was great. Then came the letter saying somebody else had better qualifications." She sighs.

"I'm exhausted running my own business, chasing after clients, doing it all myself. I'm supporting myself and helping pay the college expenses of my two kids. I need a stable income, and it's not happening. Having been out of the job market these last seven years is killing me."

Melissa has failed. She has not found the corporate position she has been seeking for more than a year. She is deeply into the discontent side of the cycle. She *thinks* success will come—she has worked hard for it—but she doesn't know how.

As Peter Senge says, in the quote at the beginning of this chapter, failure is an opportunity for learning. Melissa is learning.

So is Lanny, who found himself with each of the three opportunities described by Senge. Like Melissa, Lanny has his own business—placing consultants in companies that need short-term computer help. Lanny sees that his maturing industry has "become crowded and brutally price competitive" and because he saw this late (inaccurate picture of current reality) his sales and profits declined. Responding to the decline, he promoted one of his top salespeople to sales manager—and sales continued their downward spiral (strategy that didn't work as expected). So Lanny returned this person to a sales territory and hired a professional sales manager, a computer whiz with IBM marketing experience, and sales are growing again. So are Lanny's leadership skills, for he now has clarity of vision (the third of the learning opportunities identified by Senge). Lanny has a new and bigger conception of this company's future and the vision is energizing everyone in the organization. Lanny failed—but he didn't fail to learn. His success grows.

Lanny will fail again, but he will not make the worst mistake of all. He will not fail to try.

Failing to Try

"When in charge," says General H. Norman Schwarzkopf, "take command." Whether we are in charge of troops or just our own lives, we are often called on to make decisions without adequate information. As a result, we may put off deciding to do anything at all. That's a big mistake, says Schwarzkopf. Decisions themselves elicit new information. "The best policy is to decide, monitor the results, and change course if necessary."

Bill is a 32-year-old grocery clerk, bored and underemployed. He is unhappy with the mindless work he does each day, but glad to have the generous pay package his union has negotiated, and dependent on their medical coverage to treat his diabetes and eye problems. His wife and two children also depend on the income and the health care.

Bill dreams of owning a record store that specializes in 78 rpm music, a place where his hobby can provide a living that provides a service for the people in his town. He has even prepared a business plan for his dream store and come up with a name, "Renaissance Records."

What is Bill doing to make his dream come true? Nothing. He is not investigating possibilities. He is not asking questions. Is there a prospective partner out there, someone who would love to help run her own "Renaissance Records" store? Is there a transitional job that might lead to his dream? Is there a way to continue his health care if he leaves his clerking job? What does he *really* want? Is there a dream behind his dream, a dream more ready to come true than "Renaissance Records"? Until Bill makes the effort, none of these questions will be answered. Until Bill fails, he will not succeed—except in keeping the boring, demeaning job he has now.

No matter how insurmountable the obstacles we face, no matter how severe our financial problems, there is always some action we can take to help move us out of our discontent.

> **Success Strategy: Fail Often.** Make lots of mistakes in pursuit of your vision. Be active, active, active in both doing and learning if you want your dreams to come true.

Faces of Failure

Like Hydra, the many-headed mythological monster, failure has many faces. Sometimes big, sometimes small. Sometimes disquieting, sometimes terrifying. The face of failure changes as we come to know it. The face changes as we turn failure into an ally.

Sometimes we make the wrong job choice, sometimes we pick the wrong career. Sometimes—like Winston Churchill—we conceive a strategy that fails. All of these work out in the end if we learn by our experience. All of these work out if we become skillful at handling the human side of failure. What counts is how we handle failure.

Failure is healed by forgiveness, in three sequential steps. All three are essential if we want to strengthen relationships while learning from our mistakes.

1. **Forgive yourself.** You will make mistakes in pursuit of your purpose. Accept them. You will take wrong turnings, sometimes for the wrong reasons. That's okay. There is a way back to the right road and you will find it faster if you quit blaming yourself. I speak from experience: beating up on myself is a habit I picked up long ago. I'm breaking the habit and, if you have it, I hope you are, too.

2. **Forgive others.** Once you forgive yourself, you can forgive others. Once you forgive others, you can forgive yourself and live in the compassionate cycle of forgiveness. We all remember mistakes, ours and some made by others, but we can forgive them. We can release them. Which is wondrously liberating because miracles emerge from forgiveness.

3. **Seek forgiveness.** When you wrong others, talk to them. Be specific about your mistake. Demonstrate that you understand and explain what went wrong. Practice humility. Apologize. Ask: "How can I make this right?" and listen for the answer. Ask: "Will you forgive me?"

There are whole books written on forgiveness, and for good reason. But if you can practice the three steps just described, you will be rewarded by miracles. "They say best men are molded out of faults," Shakespeare wrote 400 years ago, "and, for the most part, become much more the better for being a little bad."

Rising from the Ashes

Like the fabled Phoenix in Greek mythology, we can rise from our own ashes. The fire of failure can spark new life.

Melissa found new life in her own business after failing to find a corporate job. She talked to former clients who gave her encouragement, support, and new referrals. Suddenly she has more business than ever before—and lots more income than a paycheck would provide. "It's a whole new game," says Melissa. "It's like I'd been reborn."

Churchill was reborn after the Dardanelles debacle—several times. Though defeated for Parliament in *five* elections, he persevered. Though defeated in many battles, he persevered—and won the war. In admiring Churchill's tenacity and creativity, one cabinet minister said that he "would gladly listen to 50 of Winston's outlandish ideas because out of the hodge-podge would always emerge one gem." If one of the world's great minds had 49 failures for each success, perhaps you and I are doing better than we thought.

EXPLORATION: What Have I Learned from Failure? Make a list of your failures and mistakes. Beside each note what you have learned from it. How will you live differently for having done this exploration?

CHAPTER

26

Reaching Out

Sentiment without action is the ruin of the soul. One brave deed is worth a thousand books.

—Edward Abbey

Smile. Greet people. Make people feel comfortable. Imagine that you are the host in every room that you enter and make people feel welcome.

—Susan RoAne, *How to Work a Room*

Since nobody is quite sure why we were put on this earth in the first place, I suppose we might as well have as good a time as we can.

—Herb Caen, column, October 6, 1992

At a holiday party with longtime friends, I see a group of people gathered near the fireplace. They are listening to Elana Rosen, I soon discover, as she sits curled up by the coffee table talking about her role in creating a public television documentary on Czeslaw Milosz, a Lithuanian-born Polish poet who won the 1980 Nobel Prize for literature.

Sparkling with passion, Elana describes the challenge of getting the right people to the right places with the right equipment and helping to make it all happen. At age 27, one of the youngest to serve as an associate producer in public television, she speaks with both authority and passion.

What will come out of this moment? Something significant, I'll bet, something magic. Those present include educators, attorneys, authors, executives, and other professionals. They range in age from 17 to 95, men and women who could help Elana get more of the television work she dearly loves.

As Elana connected with those gathered that day, as the passion of her work inspired each listener, she was moving her dream toward reality in ways she could not even guess. She was responding to her emotions, moved by her enthusiasm, without knowing where it might lead. Elana was excited, and she took the risk of expressing that excitement to those around her.

Reach Out

Those of us who aspire to lives that have meaning and value cannot do it by ourselves—we need help. To get help, we need to reach out. One way is with our enthusiasm and excitement, like Elana Rosen. What could be better than to let your light shine whenever you are inspired? Especially if your reaching out is part of an organized approach.

Being organized means thinking about purpose. It means knowing what you want . . . while staying receptive to new information that could alter your course. Being purposeful means exploring all the time, not just when you are at the exploration stage in your life cycle. It involves having a plan for reaching out to others, a plan that can include:

- Talking to people at parties (while staying within the conversational rules of the group).
- Walking down the hall at work to let a co-worker know what you are up to (while keeping your time commitment to your employer).
- Conversations at professional lunch and dinner meetings, even those where business talk is officially discouraged.
- Meeting people at classes and workshops and letting them know what you are about.

- Meeting people at religious services (while being sensitive to unwritten rules about when and where to talk shop).
- Connecting with people *wherever* two or more are gathered together, and inviting them to reach out to you, too.

Modern technology provides us with many other ways to reach out, including:

- The telephone, which even reaches people on the highway and in swimming pools. Calling is not expensive and can bring quick results (some executives make or take more than 100 calls a day). Call to ask advice, to get a lead on someone else to call, to keep a friend informed, to say thanks. When there is a live person on the other end of the line, you get instant feedback, which has value even if the feedback is negative.
- Voice mail and answering machines, which give very little information back but will listen without interrupting to whatever message you want to leave. Fast, accurate, inexpensive, voice mail is given high ratings by senior executives.
- Fax machines, another use for telephone lines, provide instant contact in writing. You can send a picture, chart, or graph as well as words.
- Audio tapes, which can be used to send a personal message or let a friend hear an inspiring speaker whose presentation has moved you.
- Video tapes, which require more elaborate equipment than audio tapes. Like audio tapes, video is a medium for either a personal or professionally done message. To increase viewership, send along a bag of popcorn.
- Modem communications, which link many computer owners.
- Video phones, which will soon be more widely available.

If all else fails, you can run an ad in the classified section of the newspaper, as this man did:

> Well educated, middle-aged in-
> telectual [his spelling, not mine]
> seeks decent paying work. Noth-
> ing too heavy, too dirty, or too
> illegal, please. Call George at . . .

Effective communicators use both the written and spoken word, paying attention to both graceful expression and correct spelling. They phone and follow up with a letter, or fax an agenda before a conference call, or add a handwritten Post-it note to a proposal. They use desktop publishing to make résumés, reports, and bios more readable and attractive than ever before possible.

Jamie used desktop publishing to create a Personal Business Plan. His name, address, and phone number appeared at the top, followed by his mission statement: "To Excel at Commercial Real Estate Sales." The plan then listed strategies. The first was "Build Experience Base," and there it listed full- and part-time selling successes. The second was "Continue to Learn," and there Jamie listed his college degree and real estate courses. The third strategy was "Contact Real Estate Leaders," which Jamie did, using most of the connecting techniques listed here (he mailed or faxed more than 100 of his Business Plans). The result? After 22 interviews, many with company presidents, he got the job he was seeking.

What all this means is that there are lots and lots of ways to reach out to people. Often you will meet rejection, and sometimes you will be discouraged. Sometimes you will have to try more than once, using several communication technologies, to reach the right person. The rewards—the desired results and pleasant surprises and joyful connections—make the effort worthwhile.

Stay Connected

The way to be effective in reaching out to people in your work life is to maintain your human, spiritual, and philosophical connections. Just as the tree needs deep roots if its branches are to reach high, so you and I need a good earth connection to sustain our outreach.

There are three main connections to sustain:

• **The Vision Connection.** Lose your dream and the next thing you know you've lost direction. As you move through the cycles of your life, keep asking: What is this all about? What is my purpose? What is my mission? Reaching out becomes onerous without a purpose, and when reaching out declines, results decline too. Our philosophy in life keeps us going, even when it's not totally clear to us. Our spiritual connections, one to another and to something larger than all of us, make the effort worthwhile.

• **The Family and Friends Connection.** Those who know us best, warts and all, offer honest feedback and deep nurturing. Their love is the best love, the most enduring. Their words can be the most insightful, even when they hurt, because usually that means they see in us what we don't want to face. These days when I get angry with my brother I say, "Whoa! Now that I've erupted, now that I've had my emotional charge, what can I learn from this?" I don't always remember to thank him for what he teaches me, but I always appreciate it. And I stay connected.

• **The Coach, Counselor, Mentor Connection.** We get a mother whether we want one or not. But usually we have to take the initiative to get a coach, counselor, or mentor. We have to go out for the team, look in the Yellow Pages under "career counselors," or otherwise seek help. When our need is most urgent we usually find a way to connect. When the need diminishes it is important to manage the transition with skill, to say good-bye with clarity and compassion. Whatever we say, it is advisable to keep our coaches, counselors, and mentors informed of our lives and our progress, to maintain the potential for new connections in the future. In my life, the longest mentor connection goes back 40 years to my junior high school basketball coach, a wonderful man whom I still write and visit. John Whitacre showed me how to excel, in sports and in life, and I make sure he knows how much he is appreciated.

Success Strategy: Manage your connections. Keep your address book, Rolodex, mailing lists, and computer files current. Add to the book in which you record birthdays and anniversaries. Let people know you care.

In September 1989, the headline in our local daily read "Seeing the USA the Hard Way." It was a story about 20 men and women who were planning to run across the country in relays to raise money for drug abuse prevention. Transcon '89 seemed like a good idea, but what really got my attention was when I read that one of the runners was Terry Pearce.

Looking back on that moment, I realize that my friend Terry became part of that adventure because he is good at what this chapter urges. Terry reaches out to lots and lots of people, including one of those who organized this cross-country event. And he knows how to stay connected—to his passion for physical fitness, to his concern about drug abuse, to his dedication to serving society.

I aspire to be like Terry Pearce, in reaching out and staying connected, and I hope you do, too. I intend to do something about it, starting today. I hope you will, too.

PART

V

Living on Purpose

27

High on Work

Neither do men light a candle, and put it under a bushel, but on a candlestick; and it giveth light unto all that are in the house.

Let your light so shine before men, that they may see your good works, and glorify your father, which is in heaven.

—Matthew 5:15-16

You can't eat for eight hours a day nor drink for eight hours a day nor make love for eight hours a day—all you can do for eight hours a day is work. Which is the reason why man makes himself and everybody else so miserable and unhappy.

—William Faulkner

An individual has to find what electrifies and enlivens his own heart, and wakes him.

—Joseph Campbell

"A Monday through Friday sort of dying," is how Studs Terkel described it in *Working*. Many of those he interviewed about work were even more expressive:

Hub, a crane operator: "If you're out there eating dust and dirt for eight, ten hours a day, even if you're not doing anything, it's work. Just *being* there is. . . ."

Nora, a staff writer: "This is the first comfortable job I've ever had in my life and it's absolutely despicable."

Mike, a steelworker: "What does an actor do when he's got a bad movie? I've got a bad movie every day."

Pauline, movie critic: "I've spent most of my life working at jobs I hated . . . at boring office jobs . . . that exhausted my spirit and energy."

Booker, former seaman: "It's impossible to pay for the loss of family life. The time away is like being in jail."

And yet many people find joy in their work. Mihaly Csikszentmihalyi (the psychologist from the University of Chicago who is studying "flow") tested workers at five companies in the Chicago area. He and the co-author of his study, Judith LeFeure of USC, discovered that while respondents "have much more positive feelings at work than in leisure," they typically said that they wished they weren't working.

There is massive evidence that people have "positive feelings" at work. Even in Terkel's book, barbers, cab drivers, real estate brokers, and many others have good things to say about the work they are doing. How can we have positive feelings more of the time? Is the answer to create, individually and in groups, more of what makes us feel good at work?

People Highs

Even the most cynical acknowledge the value of social interactions at work. The human connections, the shared joys, and the laughter cut our loneliness. Sure, there is conflict, competition, and gossip at work; but most of the time most of us like to work with other people.

In fact, people can be part of a real high at work—and not the kind of high that comes from sipping, smoking, snorting, or shooting, but the natural high of elevated energy levels and psychic juice. This high is the transcendent joy that lifts us above self-consciousness and mundane concerns. It is wonderful, exuberant—and doesn't cost a cent.

People highs come when two or more create an exciting plan, make a breakthrough on a tough problem, or arrive at a major accomplishment. It can come on the way to any of these, or when people come together afterward to celebrate. What we are talking about here is being high with other people for a magic moment, or magic hour, and sharing the afterglow, sometimes for years.

People highs are one of the best memories for Terry Pearce, the cross-country runner I introduced in the last chapter. Charged with high hopes and high energy, Transcon '89 was an emotionally charged experience for all 20 runners and their support team right from the start.

"The first real high was the day we said we were actually going to do it," Terry says, remembering the group decision to try for a world record while raising money for drug abuse prevention. "None of us would have done it alone . . . the decision made us a family. There was the feeling of anxiety, like before stepping over the cliff. I was gulping hard, with tears starting in my eyes."

The second big high for Terry was the day the run started. "I knew three or four runners, but most I had never met—it was the first time the whole team came together, people from all over the country, bound together by a certain craziness, all in the same uniforms. There in the staging area were ten RVs and a truck full of food, all the things that were going to feed and care for us for the next 3,015 miles."

How did it feel?

"Oh, shit! *Really* good! I felt lots of pride, pride in the human spirit. Here we all were, about to do it, even though we knew it was costing everyone tremendous resources, investments of flesh, money, time."

Was this run really work? It qualifies on the basis of BTUs burned, about 5,000 a day for each of the 20 runners. It was work in the way that physics defines work, and it was work if you agree with me that work includes all productive, creative activity. If work must be organized and planned, this qualifies. It even qualifies for those who think that in order to be work it must make money: the event raised thousands of dollars for drug abuse prevention, even though none of the runners was "paid."

Joane Bumpus, a veteran of 26 marathons and 23 ultramarathons, remembers her best people high on the run across the country. "It was in Illinois, the most wonderful state, where we always had a police car driving a few yards ahead of us, lights flashing. It was this sunny morning, in the middle of the state, cornfields on all sides. I come running up over a hill and there on my left is a whole school turned out, all the kids, cheering, with signs saying WE DON'T DO DRUGS."

Success Strategy: Pick your people. Team up with those who stimulate your creativity, your productivity, your sense of humor, and your moral awareness—whether you like them or not. Find new ways to work with such people.

Creativity Highs

Another wonderful high comes with creative breakthroughs. There are moments of inspiration at the computer or keyboard or loom or easel, in a meeting, or on a morning run. They are usually preceded by the struggle to solve some kind of problem, by worrying about some challenge. When the solution breaks through the clouds, joy and exuberance shine forth. One idea follows another, in a high that can last minutes—or even hours.

Terry Pearce talks about a creativity high he experienced while running through the Utah desert. "I'm running along, in full moonlight. I'm watching for rattlesnakes that crawl out on the pavement to get warm at night and I can see deer up in the foothills. I'm thinking about our efforts to get media attention, and wondering why no one is very excited about this group of world-class runners crossing the United States to break world record.

"Then it dawns on me. I'm not a world-class runner, most of us aren't. What we are is a bunch of ordinary slugs doing something extraordinary in community. When I finish my eight miles I tell the others in my RV and before long this becomes a breakthrough for the whole group, a mirror of what we are.

"We rewrite our press releases with this new idea as the headline and when we get to Hannibal fax it out to the news media." TV and newspaper coverage increased dramatically, starting the next day, with leads like this:

TRANSCON '89 ROARED INTO ILLINOIS TODAY ON THE LEGS OF 20 DIVERSE CITIZENS DETERMINED TO HELP CHANGE AMERICA'S ATTITUDES ABOUT DRUG ABUSE PREVENTION.

Terry's creativity high on the desert led to a high for the whole Transcon community, illustrating one of the rewards of highs at work—whether it's finding the right product for a customer, fixing a production line glitch, or inventing a new software drive. They often link one to the other, like overlapping circles:

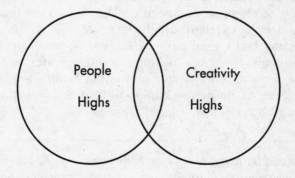

Excellence Highs

For those of us in search of it, there is nothing quite so wonderful as excellence—and the high, fine feeling when we visit that magical domain. The feeling may last only a few hours, and then we may be off in search of new realms of excellence. There is often positive feedback, in words or numbers, to tell us we have arrived, but none of that means anything if we do not recognize it ourselves. Ultimately, these highs come because we *know* we are operating in what is, for us, a realm of excellence.

Excellence is the stone mason getting a wall just right, or the airline pilot making a perfect landing. It is the executive leading a meeting that produces outstanding results, or the writer finding the exact phrase to express her thoughts. It is the tennis player serving aces, or the industrial engineer delving into a complex problem for the perfect answer. It is Michael Jordan in the flow of a basketball game or Michael De Bakey making miracles with a scalpel.

When I was a college professor there would be 10- or 15-minute stretches of a class when we would arrive at that place called excellence; sometimes it seemed like a full class period was at that level, or even a series of classes. The feeling was heady, ecstatic, and uplifting, sometimes for days afterward, as the reality of where we had been sunk in. It took me many years to recognize the excellence highs in my life—I was into my forties and had had several before I knew what was happening.

These highs are worth looking for and definitely worth finding. They involve other people in a joyful, healthy way. There is no hangover, no guilt, no clean-up with these highs, just happy people and bushels full of good feelings.

Success Strategy: Always improve. Before age 40 improve on your weaknesses—through courses, study, training, reading, practice. After 40, improve on your strengths, aiming for excellence.

Achievement Highs

In the world of natural highs, achievement ranks right beside excellence. In fact, one often leads to the other. Achievement highs are what the fund-raiser feels when the report is submitted, the production team feels when the car is finished, the runner feels at the finish line. It is a high all of us have felt, in small ways and big ways; it is available throughout the world of work.

Achievement highs on Transcon '89 began when runners committed to the idea. Then "it built as we went across the country," according to Joane Bumpus. "Even though there were only rare moments of seeing one another, you could feel other team members validating your performance. We were cheering each other, supporting each other."

How did it feel at the finish line?

"There were hugs and jokes, lots of celebrating. We were like high schoolers when we finally arrived in Washington, signing posters for one another, scrawling mushy messages. Everywhere you could feel that there was an enormous generation of energy and respect."

There was also a new world record, of 15 days, one hour, breaking the previous record by six hours—an achievement high shared by the 20 runners and every supporter.

"When we get together now," says Terry Pearce—after the runners are back to their regular work and most of the world has forgotten what they achieved—"it's magic. We sit together and watch the video and cry, still moved and astounded that it really happened."

High on Purpose

Not everything can be planned—in work or in life—but when the right conditions are created, wonderful results can ensue, in your life and in mine. We can find people who are exciting to work with. We can pick problems that deeply engage our creativity. And we can enjoy the excellence and achievement highs that result.

If we do this in alignment with our purpose, we heighten the high. We invite the feeling of fulfillment that comes from doing what we are intended to do. We act with less hesitancy, less uncertainty, and with no upper psychological limit—no "fear of success"—to limit us.

You and I do not have to run across the United States to find highs in the work we do. The possibility is here before each of us, every day, for highs that link and overlap like petals in a flower along our path.

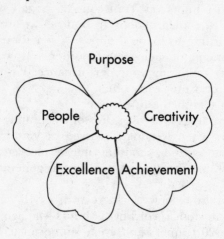

EXPLORATION: **When Do I Get High on Work?** Scan back over the last five years and list the times you got high on work. Go back 10 years now, and include all kinds of work regardless of whether you got paid. Star your best highs. Now list ways to get more of these highs in your future.

CHAPTER

28

Time for Every Purpose

To every thing there is a season and a time
to every purpose under the heaven.

—Ecclesiastes 3:1

Whoever cultivates the golden mean
avoids both the poverty of a hovel and the
envy of a palace.

—Horace

Life is like an ice cream cone—
you take it one lick at a time.

—Charlie Brown

"Many came to me privately," reports Pierre Mornell, M.D., "and
said they were very troubled by 14-hour days and six-day weeks."
Mornell is talking about IBM executives attending seminars he
led in Armonk, New York, on balancing work and personal time.
Initially, participants were stone faced. "There's a tremendous
fear of getting into these personal issues."

There is resistance among those who head companies, too.
The *Fortune* magazine article that quoted Mornell also cited a
survey of CEOs in which 77 percent said that "large U.S. companies will have to push their managers harder if we are to
compete successfully with the Japanese and other global competitors." Only 9 percent felt that U.S. companies are pushing managers too hard.

Most managers disagree. So do most working Americans,

according to Juliet Schor, author of *The Overworked American*. "My analysis concludes," says Schor, "that over the last 20 years the annual work schedule of Americans increased by 163 hours a year." This additional month of work is because there are "strong incentives on the part of employers against translating productivity increases into leisure time and in favor of using productivity increases to produce more output." But longer hours do not necessarily mean more work gets done, according to Schor. "Many managers are stuck on the idea that long equals productive," she says. "But that's not what the evidence shows."

Productivity is not rising as fast as hours worked and neither is happiness—at least not according to a Gallup Mirror of America poll, which shows that half of all workers (57 percent) say work gives them too little time to relax and "do nothing" or pursue sports, hobbies, and recreation. Nearly one in six employed adults now works a second job, according to this study, and more than one in three works regular evenings or weekends.

Polls conducted by Lou Harris & Associates also show that Americans are working more and playing less. Between 1973 and 1987 the amount of time spent at work and commuting increased 15 percent, from 40.6 hours to 46.8 hours, and leisure hours dropped 37 percent, from 26.2 hours a week to 16.6 hours a week. Everywhere there is evidence that work is consuming us.

Time pressures, real and imagined, are greater than ever and there seems no letup in sight. With more two career couples and new technology every day to help us work more intensely, where is all this going to end? Whatever happened to balance?

The Golden Mean

There is a happy balance point between the hovel and the palace, as Horace reminds us, and also between sleep and awake time, between active and quiet time, between work and play. Those who live best do not have too much work or too much play. They find the right amount of love and learning, the right amount of solitude and exercise.

Finding the golden mean requires planning, creativity, and compromise. If you want to meet a friend for breakfast but it's a morning you usually work out, maybe you can go for a run together in the park. If you need to work late Monday night, plan to go home early on Tuesday. If you must make a choice between two activities that are important to you, do it based on consciously chosen priorities.

How do experts find balance in their lives? Consider Pierre Mornell, the psychiatrist who conducts seminars on the topic. "I do different work each day," he says, "which helps keep the balance and minimize the boredom. I'm traveling less these days and riding my bike more."

Mornell is also quick to admit that he does not have it all figured out yet. "At ten o'clock on a Saturday night just a few weeks ago," he says with a smile, "I was in Los Angeles, 500 miles from my family, talking on the telephone with a colleague about balance, and we broke out laughing at the irony of two experts talking on that topic at that hour."

Most of the time Mornell travels with his wife; his children are mainly out of the nest. Several years ago he and his wife bought an old house a few miles from where they live and remodeled it into an office and consulting facility where they now see clients and—when inspired—each other. "I'm still working on balance," admits Mornell. "One thing I know for sure: it takes considerable discipline and lots of planning."

Balance

If you have a spouse who works down the hall from you and if the two of you travel together, you may find time for every purpose ... at least the important ones. But balance is not easy— even for experts. It requires thought, discussion, and tough choices. It requires integrating the work part of life with play, love, and learning. It requires asking the right questions:

• **Love.** How much time do you make for those closest to you? How do you decide when there is a choice between your spouse and your children? How do you balance all that with time spent with other family members and friends? Do you find ways to bring those you love into your work life—without using that as a way to work more? Do you take time to develop friendships at work, meeting your social needs as you earn money? Do you make an effort to meet new people? Do you make yourself accessible for new friendships? Do you talk about these issues with those you care for?

• **Play.** How much time do you make for play and frivolity? Do you balance structured play, such as golf and tennis, with other games where winning is not important? Do you play indoor games, like bridge and poker and dominoes, as well as outdoor games? Do you look for activities that refresh and renew you? Do you allow yourself to be foolish, once in a while, in attire or behavior? Do you laugh at least once a day? Does your play give you physical exercise, even if it only involves walking? Juvenal, writing 1,900 years ago, extolled *mens sana in corpore sano,* "a sound mind in a sound body." If you don't know how to keep your body sound, or if you don't know how to play as well as you would like, now is the time to learn. You don't have to be a frolicaholic to have fun!

• **Learning.** How much time do you make for learning? How much effort do you make to learn from your daily experience, good and bad? How well do you learn from those around you? How skillful are you at asking to be taught? What use do you make of training courses or seminars offered where you work? How about seminars or workshops offered outside of work? Should you be taking courses to accumulate credits toward earning a degree? Should you be reading more? Listening to or viewing educational tapes? Remember the words of the philosopher and keep a sound mind by continuing to learn your whole life long.

Success Strategy: Treasure time, for it is your most valuable resource, more precious than energy, ideas, or money. Savor time. Treat it with the utmost respect.

If you want to use time more wisely, turn back to Chapter 16 and do the life-planning exercise that integrates work, love, play, and learning. Take the plan you create and tape it on the refrigerator door or on the wall beside your bed. Look at it daily.

Notice the Numbers

The more years I accumulate the more I respect those who say each one is significant. I respect time in all denominations, but I especially honor the milestone ages, those made meaningful by practice or by sages, particularly these seven:

(13) The year for religious cultural initiation from childhood into the world of adults.

(18) The year of first voting and other important rights, our second major transition into adulthood. It is the year we get full control of our lives.

(35) The middle year in our life, according to psychologist Carl Jung, when we shift from living according to the values of others and begin marching to our own drummer.

(49) Our Jubilee Year, according to biblical law, when we give everything back to God. In practice, in my own life and others I see, this is the year of letting go—who we are is no longer our position or possessions.

(65) The year we officially retire—except that if we have become free spirits we may be engaged by stimulating activities that continue for many moons more.

(99) The age of Job when his adventures started—an age of wisdom for all of us to respect and some of us to achieve.

(120) The age of Job when he died.

Notice where you are in this proud progression and what each of these years means to you. Notice how purpose in your life is different at each stage.

Remember the Mirror

As you look in the mirror each morning consider the face of the person you see there and ask about time. Is my life out of kilter with too much work? Am I spending enough time with those I love? Am I living each day with the awareness that friends die and children grow up? Am I taking care of my health? Am I happy with the person I see looking back at me?

The author of *All I Really Need to Know I Learned in Kindergarten,* Robert Fulghum, spoke recently in an auditorium near my home. He invited the audience to ask questions before his talk, so he would be sure to get them all answered and so they wouldn't be distracted trying to remember them until the end.

"There is one question I always want to ask at moments like this," he told us. " 'What is the meaning of life?' " Since none of us had asked him that, he told this story. Fulghum had asked his meaning-of-life question several times over the years, he said, and never found a satisfactory answer. Then, after a lecture one evening, he put it to an Italian philosopher.

"When I was a young boy," the philosopher replied, "in the closing months of the Second World War, German soldiers were retreating in vast numbers through our country. One night, in the little village where I lived, a German motorcycle driver came racing down our only street and just past the last house spun off the road to his death.

"The boys of the village all went out the next morning. The body was gone, and the motorcycle, but in scouring the area where it had landed, I found a piece of glass, apparently from a rearview mirror on the motorcycle, which had broken in the crash." At this point in the story, Fulghum takes out his wallet, opens it, removes a shard of mirror, and holds it up for the audience to see.

"The philosopher told us that he soon discovered something wonderful about that little piece of mirror, which was his most prized possession as a poor boy in a poor town. He found that he could use it to direct the sun's rays into cracks and crevices which had known only blackness before. He used that mirror to reflect light into dark places. That, he told us then as I tell you now, is the meaning of life."

EXPLORATION: How Balanced Is My Life? Make a list of what you need to do more of in your life. Make another of what you need to do less of. Beside each item, note what you intend to do about it, and by when.

29

Family and Other Ties

> No man is an island, entire of itself; every man is a piece of the continent, a part of the main; if a clod be washed away by the sea, Europe is the less, as well as if a promontory were, as well as if a manor of thy friends or of thine own were; any man's death diminishes me, because I am involved in mankind; and therefore never send to know for whom the bell tolls; it tolls for thee.
>
> —John Donne

"Might I be in your next book?" my friend Bob asked. It seemed like a reasonable request to me. See what you think.

Fortune, Forbes, and *The Wall Street Journal* have all written about Bob and his exemplary business success, the apex of which was the Silicon Valley start-up he took from 6 employees to 2,200, earning investors $66 for every one risked, all in just five years. Of his many awards, Bob was proudest of being named northern California "Entrepreneur of the Year" right after he sold the company.

Prior to his extraordinary business career, Bob was an exceptional student, graduating with distinction from one of the world's great universities. At the Harvard Business School he was a Baker Scholar. He had a quick wit and loved to laugh; when he told Monty Python stories he got all the accents right.

Behind the achievement and acclaim lay the shadow side of success. Bob regularly worked 70-hour weeks and usually missed seeing his children's soccer games. He found it easier to mentor young men at the office than to spend weekends at home. His work brought bank account riches to his wife and children but left them yearning for the riches of human contact.

Bob and his wife lived across the hall from my wife and me in student housing in Cambridge in the early 1960s, where he and I and another classmate teamed up on a term project for Sales Management class. We need more detail, Bob said, more charts, more numbers. I was awed by his capacity for concentration and hard work as he and I typed all night on two rented IBM Selectrics in his smoke-filled apartment to produce a 150 page report.

Then we lost touch for a few years. I knew that Bob had taken a job with a prestigious consulting firm after graduation and then moved to a major manufacturing company. "They sent us to Dallas," his wife told me later, "and in four years Bob turned an operation losing $4 million a year into one earning $16 million. He worked all the time. We hardly ever saw him."

The major manufacturing company promoted Bob back to headquarters and a vice-presidency. It didn't work out. "He tended to annoy people," is how one observer expressed it, "he asked too many questions." A year later Bob was looking for something to run, perhaps something small, ideally in California. Which is when he left big-company security to accept the presidency of the tiny, struggling venture that grew into the great success of his life. There were challenges right from the start, beginning with a lawsuit by a huge competitor. "We all went to court," his wife told me, "the whole family, all four kids, and sitting there were 15 pinstripe lawyer types for the other side." Bob and his company won that one, when the judge was riled by the intimidation tactics of Bob's giant opponent.

Bob was perfect in his new job, according to an attorney who worked with him, because he was:

- unbelievably smart
- committed
- hard working
- tenacious
- analytical

- driven irrevocably to success and willing to give every last ounce of himself to reach that goal

Bob's drive for success led ultimately to the sale of his company, producing millions for his investors and himself, in his fortieth year. When he left the organization, three years later, Bob presented some 50 people with whom he had worked closely a copy of *Jonathan Livingston Seagull* as a "small, symbolic personal gift." Each book was inscribed and in one that went to a cofounder, Bob wrote about the early days.

Remember our simplified motives?
1. Have fun.
2. Build something important of which we can be proud.
3. Make lots of money.

Then

We made it!

Bob planned to do some consulting with "the balance of my time reserved for me and my family." Travel and biking and a second home in the wine country were part of this plan, which lasted just two months before Bob returned to the fast track, joining four corporate boards and accepting the presidency of another start-up company. "Bob did an enormous amount of planning in business," his wife told me, "but zero personally." Bob was back to working hard and once again the time for himself and his family shrank.

The start-up company had some initial success, then it shrank, too. "Everything Bob touched had turned to gold," says one of his colleagues there, "and our failure was hard on him ... though he never lost his sense of humor."

Bob's new wealth was hard on him, too. "He had a lot of paranoia about the money," his wife told me. "He started reading Howard Ruff doomsday letters, got fanatical about storing food in the garage, and worried about the children being kidnapped."

For our twenty-fifth graduate school reunion commemorative

book, Bob wrote "Health is good; life is fine; we are happy." But he and his wife missed the reunion because, we were told, a spot had been discovered on his lung. In a letter to me 10 months later, the one in which he asked about being included in this book, Bob said that he had "started out of the dark days" and that:

> The removal of half my lung and then extensive radiation treatments knocked me flat. I fought back by giving up smoking, pursuing positive thoughts, exercising regularly, and spending time with family. This week I passed my one-year-from-diagnosis milestone, so I am one of the 5% first year survivors. Now to be one of the 2% second year and 1% third year survivors.

Bob loved to gamble, in business and in Las Vegas, so he knew about odds and he knew about winning and losing. It was in Bob's fiftieth year, in the home where he and his family had lived since coming to California, that he lost his battle with cancer.

"He smoked two packs a day," his wife told me. "At the end he became very guilty about cigarettes. When his health went bad, he felt like he had missed a lot." She lowered her eyes. "He didn't take time for himself and his family."

How do the kids feel? "They feel kind of cheated. They would have liked more time." And finally: "I had great respect for what he could do and I feel a great sadness for what he missed. I loved him dearly."

In his letter to me Bob wrote:

> I am a late bloomer in the "leisure time" and "hobby" areas, but I am a very quick study. Looking back, I have no idea how I found time to work! Does all this qualify as a "second career"?

So this is for you, Bob, and to all career changers, with love and respect. This is for all who find value in your life as they read the story you invited me to tell.

Family

In the great sea of humanity, no man is an island. No woman either, and no child. Each is a part of the whole, whether we see it or not, connected by mothers, fathers, and grandparents, by brothers, sisters, spouses, children, lovers, and friends. The turns in our lives affect others, in big ways and small.

My friend Bob was talented, loving, and "a driven man who gave life everything he had," in the words of one who worked with him. He gave his family status, security, and companionship—but not as much time as they would have liked.

Bob, like all who work, faced choices. He faced time choices: whether to take the extra hour on a crucial project or have dinner with the family, whether to be in New York to meet with a banker or in California for his daughter's birthday. He faced commitment choices: was he more committed to the success of a business or to the success of the family unit he headed? He faced health choices: was work more important than a balanced life that included exercise, recreation, and healthy habits?

We are all social animals and work is a social activity, even when we do it by ourselves. There are always choices, sometimes hard ones, and trade-offs. Finding our way down the middle road is never easy.

Compromise

The word means co-promise. Compromise, to promise together, when two or more people come to an agreement that leads to action, which is more difficult than it sounds when real people face real issues in the real world. If you doubt it, try playing Solomon with each of these scenarios:

- An IBM sales executive, age 34, wants to leave Big Blue and start her own company marketing used computers. Her husband, age 38, is concerned that his salary as a teacher may not take them through the time needed to build her business.

- A former military pilot, age 42, wants to accept a job flying crop-duster planes. His wife is worried about the high mortality rate among crop-duster pilots and not at all sure the extra income is worth the risk.
- A retired civil servant, age 55, wants to spend a year traveling in Europe with his wife. She is an advertising agency executive, age 42, and reluctant to abandon a satisfying and well-paying job.
- A successful television personality, age 36, is offered a major job in another city at twice her current pay. Her husband, committed to his growing business, and her young children, do not want to move and hate the idea of her being 500 miles away five days a week.
- Your own scenario.

There are no easy answers when facing choices like these, but there are questions that can lead to the formulation of satisfying compromises. Try them in this order:

1. What do I want? Make a list, the longer the better. Include specifics about time, money, meaning, joy. Include short-term wants but also your longer-term deep desires. After you have listed everything you can possibly think of, put a red star beside the items that are most important to you.
2. What does the other person want? Encourage them to make a list, as you have done, and red star the most important items. If there are children or other family members involved, encourage them to do the same.
3. Write down the goals you agree on, such as finding satisfying work or sending the children to college.
4. How strongly do we each feel about the items we do not have in common? Go back to your want list and code every item. M = Must Have, W = Would Like to Have, G = Giveaway, not that important. Compare lists and discuss.
5. What options do we have for compromise? Be flexible with this, be creative and outrageous. List as many possibilities as you can conceive of. Look at time trade-offs, now versus later, more versus less. Look at money trade-offs, places to

save or borrow, ways to make do with less. Pick an option you agree on. Develop a plan to make it happen.

This may not be the time for you to go through this full five-step process. When the time comes, though, this is a process that works.

Success Strategy: Use Purpose as a Connecting Point. Use your understanding of what you are here for as a way to talk with those you love. Bring purpose into your negotiations. Be clear and open about your intent. Discuss life direction—yours and others—in arriving at compromises.

We never make work decisions in a vacuum, solely by ourselves. There are always others to consider. Yet each of us is ultimately responsible for our own choices. We are all ultimately responsible for our own lives.

> . . . and therefore never send to know
> for whom the bell tolls; it tolls for thee.

CHAPTER
30
Practice Gratitude

Each has his own special gift from God,
one of one kind and one of another.

—1 Corinthians 7:7

So much has been given to me; I have no
time to ponder over that which has been
denied.

—Helen Keller

We grow in love as we grow in
gratefulness. We grow in gratefulness as
we grow in love.

—Brother David Steindl-Rast

High over the Mediterranean on the western end of Sicily sits
the ancient village of Erice. On the best situated promontory of
the mountain, just south of the village, lies a temple to the Greek
goddess of love, Aphrodite. Ancient mariners came from Thebes
and Rhodos and Corinth to worship at this temple. My wife and
I came from Palermo.

Though little remains of the temple now, the spirit of the
goddess is strong in Erice. We found a small ristorante for dinner
and spent the night in an old hotel, chilled by the March mountain winds. The cold had us up at dawn, and as I fumbled
around for my socks part of me was still in a dream from the
night before.

In this dream I am facilitating a meeting of top corporate

managers working together on interpersonal problems. I think of all I will get these executives to say, and see myself putting it up on newsprint. I worry some that my agenda isn't full enough, but all in all, it is a happy, positive dream.

"Pre-cognitive!" I wrote in my journal that spring morning in 1987. "I'd like to do such work." I knew I was leaving college teaching and I thought I'd do some business consulting, but I had no inkling that four years later I would be leading a group of 12 corporation presidents working on interpersonal and other business problems. We use an easel, as in the dream, and I worry about having a full agenda, though it has never been a problem.

Did the goddess visit me with a vision that night on the mountain in Erice? Did my waking dream somehow merge with a dream from my sleep to give me a view of the future? I don't expect to find the answers, but I know that I treasure those hours at the temple. And every time I remember the experience, I feel enormous gratitude.

Gratitude for Dreams

Of all the things to be grateful for, what could be more important than our dreams, hopes, and aspirations—even the dreams that come to us in the night. Without such dreams, hopes, and aspirations, our energy and talent take us nowhere. Without a vision, we are mired in aimlessness and despair.

Whether yours is a big dream or a small one, honor it. Whether it is for the whole planet or for the job you hope to be offered next week, respect it. Whether it is clear or shining or vague and fuzzy, it is of value. If you are not happy with your dream, start by accepting it just as it is—and then go to work to build a bigger dream that you like better.

Express gratitude by writing out your dreams, whether they come in the day or in the night. Respect them and nurture them. When the time is right—and only you will know when that is—tell others of your dreams. Put them into spoken words. Let them out into the light of day so that others can be inspired in pursuit of their own dreams and join you in pursuit of yours.

Gratitude for Gifts

Your own special gift is different from mine and different from the gifts of your family and friends. Our challenge, yours and mine, is to find our gifts, to discover and develop the talent, knowledge, and passion we have for making a difference in the world.

The search for one's gifts, like the search for self-knowledge, is lifelong. It is a philosophical search, but it is also practical, starting with questions like: What do I do well? What do I know? What do I care most about? Given enough time and sharp pencils, any of us can learn a lot more than we know now about our talent, knowledge, and passion.

We can give thanks for our gifts: a silent "Thank you" or "Thank you, God" can work wonders. We can also give thanks for gifts we *don't* have, attributes that would change our lives in negative ways. But the best way to give thanks for our gifts is to go out and use them, to put them to work in the real world.

> **Success Strategy: Be Patient with Purpose.** It becomes clear in its own time. Keep looking. Expect success. But don't be surprised if insights come in ways you did not anticipate.

Gratitude for Setbacks

"Dear John," the letter begins. "We have carefully considered your qualifications." And? "We feel that there are others more qualified than you." Oooof! A boot in the belly. "We will, however, keep your letter on file." Lord knows where, though, or how anyone would ever find it again, or want to. "Thank you for your interest." Sure, and thank you for obliterating my day.

Then out of the pain, rising on wings from the ashes, comes hope: an idea for another company to write, the inspiration to make the next phone call, the motivation to ask a friend for help. Yes, she says, we would like to meet with you; yes, I know a company that needs people like you; yes, I can help you. Yes, you hear, yes. Yes.

The boot in the belly forgotten, hope returns. Possibilities live. And somewhere behind the sternum, warm and suffusing, glows a feeling of gratitude.

Not that setbacks aren't hard. They are. Not that they don't take time to get over. They do. Wounds heal over time, in some cases lots of time, and there are wounds we never fully recover from. But we always have a choice. We can, if we decide, emerge stronger and wiser and, ultimately, grateful for all of the experiences that come into our lives.

There comes a time, usually, when we get enough distance from our setbacks to have some appreciation for them. One way to test this is to tell others about our hard times, to see how honest we can be about them and to see if there really is some appreciation. I'm willing to tell just about anyone that in the 24 years I was an employee, I was criticized, chastised, penalized, pushed out, and fired. Talking about those times helps me to understand them, but also strengthens the human bond with others who have endured similar setbacks. My appreciation feeds theirs.

It almost always helps to tell someone else, as I saw in a career change workshop I led a while back.

"These last few months have been awful," a middle-aged man told us. "It's hell being a minister and knowing you need to change but not knowing how." His problems seemed insurmountable but as he talked, the dream of heading a social service agency emerged, a job for which he was magnificently qualified. What was missing? He knew: "I need to take the plunge."

At this, all 20 of us left the meeting room, trooped down to the swimming pool, and formed a circle of support there at the edge as our minister friend stripped to his shorts. We wished him well. We assured him that he would find success. We applauded his courage. He smiled, had one last look at our supportive faces, hesitated for a moment, and then took the plunge.

> **Success Strategy: Laugh Often.** Take your work seriously, not yourself. Be aware of your emotions but don't cling to them. Smile. Smell the roses.

Gratitude for Success

Discontent can lead to wonderful success. And if you have had setbacks along the way, victory is all the more sweet.

We can practice gratitude with big successes, and small ones, too. Getting a job, completing a major project, or the first airing of a TV commercial are big successes, worth appreciating. Smaller successes, little objectives achieved, also count: the résumé newly printed, the appointment made, the letter written. Take time in your busy life to smell the sweetness of success.

Celebrate success and join others in doing the same. Celebrate by taking a moment to savor small accomplishments or by bringing friends together to toast large ones. Let people know about your successes so they can share in the good feelings and congratulate you in their own way. Congratulate others on their successes, with cards, phone calls, flowers, or banners. Put stickers on your notes that say SUPER! Laud your friends, applaud them, cheer them on.

A company president talked recently about one way he expresses gratitude: "I keep a joy journal and write in it before going to bed each night. I list the things that brought me joy that day and then sign it 'Thank You' and my name." This man, who has faced enormous adversity, does this ritual with his wife and finds it helps the two of them reconnect their busy lives. "After a rough day," he said, "it puts things in perspective."

Gratitude for Perspective

Gratitude isn't automatic. It isn't always easy. Sometimes a good bit of perspective is needed before we can feel grateful. In my own life, and in my work with other people, I've identified six steps on the path to gratitude.

1. Some combination of causes provide **stimuli**.
2. Which creates an **event,** words, or deeds.
3. The event is often followed by **feelings,** often of anger, blame, resentment, disillusionment, or disappointment.
4. The feelings in time are followed by **understanding.** "Now I see why they rejected me; I might have rejected me too under those circumstances."
5. Next comes **forgiveness,** the healing moment of releasing the anger and blame. "I accept what they did, it's okay." Sometimes forgiveness happens face to face, but it does not have to.
6. Finally, there is **appreciation.** "That rejection helped make me what I am today, and I am grateful."

These six steps happen again and again in our lives, on big issues and small. On big issues we sometimes go through these steps several times: we forgive and then something brings up the feelings again, and the anger. Which is okay if we recognize that this is a cycle, like the great cycles in our lives, in which the pattern recurs:

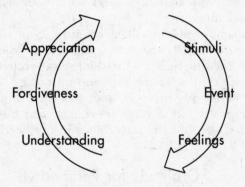

EXPLORATION: What Am I Grateful For? Take a moment to count your blessings. Think of the people who have brought good things into your life. Say thank you—with a call, a card, a dozen roses—to at least one of these people.

The Wayfarers Club

Many who travel the nation's highways belong to the Automobile Association of America, mainly because it makes the journey easier and safer. You can join another triple A, with no application forms and no fees, if you follow these three principles:

- **Anticipation.** Plan and prepare. Envision success and be ready when it arrives.
- **Alertness.** Be aware of what is going on with you, with others on the road, with the changing scene. You can't control everything that happens, but you can respond.
- **Appreciation.** Whatever arises along the way, see the good side and give thanks. Accept what you find. Acknowledge those who offer aid. Affirm yourself and others.

Anticipation, Alertness, Appreciation. If you hope to travel far on the highway of life, remember the triple A.

31

Follow Your Bliss

It's good to be just plain happy; it's a little better to know that you're happy; but to understand that you're happy and to know why and how, in what way, because of what concatenation of events or circumstances, and still be happy, be happy in the being and the knowing, well that is beyond happiness, that is bliss, and if you have any sense you ought to kill yourself on the spot and be done with it.

—Henry Miller

No one can beat you as long as you are doing your best.

—John A. Caple (1905–1979)

It's a fool's life, a rogue's life, and a good life if you keep laughing all the way to the grave.

—Edward Abbey

Joseph Campbell was single when he first taught at Sarah Lawrence College, so he often dined alone. One night at his favorite Greek restaurant a father and mother and scrawny 12-year-old came in and sat at the table next to him. Not long after the meal was served, Campbell heard the father say to the boy, "Drink your tomato juice."

"I don't want to."

"Drink your tomato juice!"

"I don't want to," the boy responds, with feeling.

Before the father can reply, the mother interrupts. "Don't make him do something he doesn't want to do."

"He's got to do what he doesn't want to do if he wants to survive," shouts the father. "My whole life I've been doing things I didn't want to do and he's darn well going to drink that tomato juice."

To Campbell, that unhappy father reflected the price paid by those who ignore their inner music and march instead to someone else's drummer. Campbell saw the pain of one disharmonious life resonating out to family and friends and anyone else in the way.

Those who spend their lives doing what other people want become brittle and dry. Their capacity for joy diminishes. They lose the ability to inspire. They exude anger and harsh words.

How many out there are like the unhappy father in the restaurant that night? Too many.

A 1988 survey of 4,126 male business executives, for instance, indicated widespread dissatisfaction at work. Based on this sampling, done by the Palo Alto Consulting Center, 48 percent of all middle managers believe that despite years spent striving to achieve professional goals, their lives are empty and meaningless. In the same study, 68 percent of senior executives said they had neglected their family lives to pursue professional goals. Half said they would spend more time with their wives and children if they could start again.

Bliss

Joseph Campbell's favorite advice was, "Follow your bliss." He recommended this path, to students and readers and lecture audiences, because it was one he himself found meaningful. He started before he was 10, heeding an impulse to study Native American culture. When he was not yet 30, he spent five years in self-directed reading and study. In his seventies, he undertook a massive trilogy on mythology, a project that engaged him to the end of his life.

Campbell talked about bliss in his 1986 interview with Bill Moyers:

> The realization of your bliss, your true being, comes when you have put aside what might be called the *passing moment* with its terror and with its temptations and its statement of requirements of life that you should live this way. . . . I always tell my students to follow their bliss—where the deep sense of being is from, and where your body and soul want to go. When you have that feeling, then stay with it, and don't let anyone throw you off. I say don't be afraid to follow your bliss and doors will open where you didn't know they were going to be.

Success Strategy: Follow Your Instincts. Act impulsively once in a while. Abandon your plan and your schedule and your responsibilities sometimes. Respond to the attractions of the moment.

Doors

"There are things that are known and things that are unknown," wrote William Blake. "In between are doors."

Doors open for us when we know where to knock, when we follow the quiet leading of our inner voices toward the unknown. Doors open for us when we knock often enough and loud enough, with authentic passion.

Doors open for those willing to make grand plans, for those courageous enough to be creative in mapping out their lives. Not all ideas become reality for such explorers—Joseph Campbell did not complete all the books he conceived—but those with the widest spectrum of possibilities and the most unthinkable ideas often end up with the most bliss.

Is it easy to know one's bliss? Rarely. In the complexity of daily lives, it is hard to find the simple course. Most of us are distracted by a cacophony of voices: old voices, new voices, then voices, now voices of parents, siblings, teachers, bosses, experts, friends. It is easy to lose our way. It is easy to forget our barely understood bliss.

Yet if our pursuit is in earnest, doors open where we didn't know there were going to be any. At every stage in the great cycles of our lives, doors open and we find that we need to move ahead. In Joseph Campbell's life doors opened to athletic achievement, to a productive academic career, to a happy marriage and, at the end, to vast new audiences for his books and lectures and interviews. For Joseph Campbell, in pursuit of his bliss, doors opened again and again throughout life's journey.

Unexpected doors can open for us too, when we follow our bliss with purity of purpose.

Purpose

To follow one's bliss is to live aligned with purpose. It is to be focused and flexible, guided and responsive. It is living true to ourselves, true to our calling, true to our vision.

To discover your bliss, think again about these seven steps to finding your purpose in life:

1. **Yearnings.** Explore the yearnings of your heart, the longings of your soul.
2. **Heroes.** Identify your heroes and heroines, those men and women you admire and emulate.
3. **Successes.** Study your life for transcendent experiences and times of fulfillment.
4. **Enthusiasms.** Ponder your values, attitudes, and beliefs for insight into what motivates you.
5. **Choices.** Look into the windows of your soul for your highest goals, ideals, talents, and passions.
6. **Friends.** Ask five friends, and more is better, how they see your purpose in life.

7. **Inspiration.** Listen to your intuition, inner voices, spiritual sources. Ask: Why am I here?

Aim, like Henry Miller, to go beyond happiness. Aim for the bliss you deserve. Be open to inspiration, wherever it arises and in whatever form. Continue to look for your right work and your right direction. Listen to what life is whispering in your ear.

Live While You Have Life to Live

"Live while you have life to live," wrote Danish resistance fighter Piet Hein, "Love while you have love to give." Don't drink your tomato juice, if you don't want to, but enjoy each meal and each moment. Please. If work is love made visible, then express that love in everything you do—on the job, at home, with friends, with strangers, in celebrations. Live each day and each year so that your life is love made visible.

Think of your love like a spring flower with each petal as a piece of your love, starting at the top with *agape*—love of God. On one side is *caritas*—love for all humanity—and on the other is *philia*, which is brotherly love. On the bottom, closest to mother earth, is *eros*, sensual love. Let your love be like this flower:

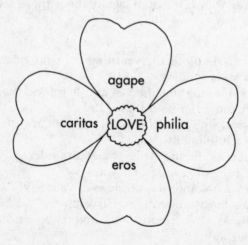

As you explore life's mountain trails, remember the heart dimension. "Work is love made visible," wrote Kahlil Gibran:

> Always you have been told that work is a curse and labor a misfortune.
>
> But I say to you that when you work you fulfill a part of the earth's furthest dream, assigned to you when that dream was born,
>
> And in keeping yourself with labor you are in truth loving life,
>
> And to love life through labor is to be intimate with life's inmost secret.

32

Toward the Infinite

In the depth of your hopes and desires lies
the silent knowledge of the beyond; and
like seeds dreaming beneath the snow
your heart dreams of spring. Trust in
dreams, for in them is hidden the gate to
eternity.

—Kahlil Gibran

Find your own wiggle,
find your own sway.
Find your own rhythm,
find your own way.

—Mary Harper

Once you place service above everything,
everything else falls in place.

—Ad for real estate brokerage

"Today I'm going to resign," I told the woman behind the bar-
ber chair, who continued snipping stray hairs over my right ear.
"I'm going to walk into the dean's office in a few minutes and
when I walk out I'll be a free man."

How could I feel so good just moments before abandoning a
tenured faculty position and 10-year career? Why did I act like a
man reprieved when I was about to sign my own death warrant
at the liberal arts college where I was a top-rated teacher?

My plan was clear, rehearsed word by word. Thank you, I

would say to the dean, for your patience with me over the years. After lots of thought and consultation, I have decided to leave the college at the end of next semester. I'm sure we can work out an equitable plan for these last three months. That will show her, I thought. Better to leave than to accept unfair punishment.

Minutes later, sitting in the dean's bleak office, tight as 10 drum heads, I blurt out my decision. "We'll be happy to give you a job cleaning classrooms," the dean says—not to me but to the job seeker whose call she takes just as I finish my rehearsed speech. The dean is concerned and patient with her caller, explaining the college philosophy in these matters: "There is always work here for those who are willing."

"Thank you for calling," says the dean, hanging up and returning to her conversation with me. She has thought about my opening words. "You know, John, you don't have to resign."

I knew. I also knew that 19 straight semesters were a lot for a stimulation junkie like me, that the four students who were unhappy with my program at Oxford University the previous summer were on to something. The waning days of a season in my life were upon me.

"Man, you done the right thing," a bearded Navy veteran told me afterwards. "Why put up with that malarkey?" He had graduated a semester before, as one of my advisees, and was in my office looking for help with his job search. He was starting a career as I was ending one—and not for the first time.

When I concluded my career in management, 14 years after earning an MBA, it was not with a bang but a whimper—three jobs, none lasting more than 18 months, all ending in failure . . . or so I thought at the time. Now I see the value of those painful days, which became the gateway to a rewarding academic career and, 10 years later, to the joyful work I do today.

My career transitions were filled with unease, uncertainty, unhappiness. With hindsight, I can see patterns and purpose in it all. I have perspective on accomplishments, setbacks, bosses, and colleagues. When I look over this littered landscape, over paths taken and not taken, over surprise successes and dreams not realized, I see a life that has meaning, for me and for those I serve. I see more than job titles and organization charts. I see human passion—ours, yours, mine—changing the world.

Love is at the heart of the richly peopled world I see, a caring about the present and the past and the future. It is "Love thy neighbor as thyself" and love the world enough to find the best in you to offer up as a gift for many to enjoy. It is the passion arising from living on purpose.

It is not all seriousness, though, but more like play—the best kind, with understandable rules, competent players, and total involvement, with fun and joy and laughter. Best of all is the pleasure that comes from moving toward mastery of the game.

Playing

In our journey toward the infinite we find how much like a game all of life is. We have objectives and uniforms and people to play with. We win, we lose, we learn in work and in life. As in any game, there are rules:

• **Rules to Learn.** Early in the game, our challenge is to learn the rules. In first jobs we discover, by watching and listening, what it takes to succeed and advance: rules of behavior, attitude, and communication. We learn where we are strong and weak, how to learn and how to persist. Usually we are working for someone else, as sustainers in established organizations, as apprentices in the world of work.

• **Rules to Make.** With self-awareness and increased confidence comes the knowledge that we participate in making the rules. We make rules for ourselves, about time management, goal setting, and relationships. We may find ourselves in leadership positions, in these middle years, and make rules with and for others. Rule makers are venturers, entrepreneurs, and organization builders, people whose joy in the game is enhanced by having control over how it is played. They often discover, with Noël Coward, that "work is more fun than fun."

• **Rules to Break.** After learning the rules and making a few, it is time for breaking rules, your own and those of the larger game. No one can break all the rules, and successful rule breakers have a strong sense of fairness, rightness, and integrity. Rule breakers may work late or early or not at all for months on end.

Rule breakers may do valuable work for no pay, or continue in challenging jobs into their eighties. Rule breakers are free spirits with a keen ear for their own inner voices. They are self-directed adventurers of the soul whose lives inspire others.

When my wife and I play dominoes, we follow rules about moving the pieces, scoring, and taking turns. We play by other rules in other parts of our lives, rules of human relationship and reality. Living rules. Relevant rules. Rules that make all the difference in how we deal with clients, associates, and each other in the bigger game called life.

The Bigger Game

In the beginning, the game is limited by our short-term goals—the next project, the next promotion, the next party. Our vision does not go much beyond those with whom we live day by day. Our focus is on achievement, on finding success, on demonstrating for ourselves and those around us that we are capable.

Once we make it—become a department head or break through some annual income barrier—our sense of the game changes. We look back on the early, narrowly focused struggles and we look ahead to larger possibilities, not just of achievement but of playing in a bigger game.

We see connections we missed earlier. We see that our pain is not ours alone. Neither is our joy. Our accomplishments are shared with those we serve and some we may never know. Our struggles and our setbacks are shared. We see that we are not alone and we recognize, with John Donne, that no man is an island.

We see the interconnectedness of our work with the work of others on the planet. Concerns for rain forests, for clean water, for the biosphere, for the environment become our concerns. The more true we are to our purpose in life, the more likely we are to recognize these things.

This bigger game embraces all people and all cultures on the planet. We may not know what impact our work has on others, but we learn to respect the fact that there is always some impact, large or small, that is part of the larger game.

The larger game becomes clear as we journey through the cycles of life, from discontent to renewal, from sustainer to free spirit. Clarity comes as we move through the steps to understanding our purpose, steps we take again and again, in a cycle that looks like this:

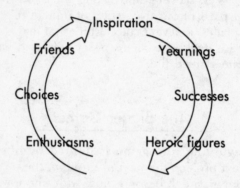

Toward the Infinite

Living on purpose creates new ideas and new energy. It brings smiles to the faces of satisfied clients and supportive friends. It puts joy in our work and enthusiasm in our hearts. It brings fulfillment to our labors and meaning to our lives.

Like the old wagon wheel leaning against a barn, those of us who live on purpose have been through many cycles. Round and round the big wheel keeps on turning, but at the hub all motion ceases—just as at the hub of all our human activity there is the quiet center of the self. As T. S. Eliot wrote, "At the still point of the turning world, there the dance is."

Where does it all end?

When we pursue our bliss, it ends in an exquisite expression of our humanity. The challenges of work fill our lives with meaning and value. Our struggles fulfill our dreams. We embark on a path that leads to frustration and to ecstasy, to heartache and to joy, to fulfillment and to bliss. In the words of Gibran:

When you work you are a flute
through whose heart the whispering of the hours
turns to music.

For to be idle
is to become a stranger unto the seasons,
and to step out of life's procession,
that marches in majesty and proud submission
towards the infinite.

MORE ON PURPOSE

For those who aspire to live on purpose here are resources for further insight & inspiration

Bolles, Dick. Author of *What Color Is Your Parachute?* (Ten Speed Press) which includes a 20+ page section on "How to Find Your Mission in Life."

Bridges, Bill (415/381-9663). Consultant on transitions and author of *Transitions* (Addison-Wesley) and *Surviving Corporate Transitions* (Wm. Bridges Associates).

Caple, John (415/457-0125). Strategic consultant and author of *The Ultimate Interview* (Doubleday) and *Finding the Hat That Fits* (Dutton, June, 1993).

Covey, Stephen. Author of *Seven Habits of Highly Effective People* (Simon & Schuster) and *Principle Centered Leadership* (Institute for Principle Centered Leadership). Call 800/331-7716 for free material on developing a personal mission statement.

Fletcher, Jerry (415/456-5200). Head of firm that helps individuals and groups develop "High Performance Patterns." Author of *Patterns of High Performance* (Berrett-Koehler, Fall, 1993).

Goodman, Lanny (505/584-7300). Strategic consultant who works with leaders on mission and purpose in Albuquerque, New Mexico.

Hudson, Frederic (805/682-3883). Head of firm doing life planning workshops in Santa Barbara and author of *The Adult Years* (Jossey-Bass).

Konstanturous, John (619/481-9043). Strategic consultant who works with leaders on mission and purpose in Del Mar, California.

Leider, Richard. Author of *The Inventurers* (Addison-Wesley) and *The Power of Purpose* (Fawcett).

Stephan, Naomi. Co-head of Life Mission Associates in L.A. and co-author of *Finding Your Life Mission Workbook* (Life Mission Associates).

RSVP

Like all who aspire to live on purpose, the author needs help, advice, criticism, encouragement. If you have any of these or suggestions for future editions of this book, please respond to:

John Caple
523 Fourth Street #206
San Rafael, CA 94901

Your purposes are important and so are your comments. I hope you will let me hear them.

INDEX